KU-271-876

South Pole

Elizabeth Leane

REAKTION BOOKS

For Zac and Tessa

Published by
Reaktion Books Ltd
Unit 32, Waterside
44–48 Wharf Road
London N1 7UX, UK

First published 2016, reprinted 2018

Copyright © Elizabeth Leane 2016

All rights reserved
No part of this publication may be reproduced, stored in a retrieval system, or transmitted, in any form or by any means, electronic, mechanical, photocopying, recording or otherwise, without the prior permission of the publishers.

Printed and bound in China by 1010 Printing International Ltd

A catalogue record for this book is available from the British Library

ISBN 978 1 78023 596 7

CONTENTS

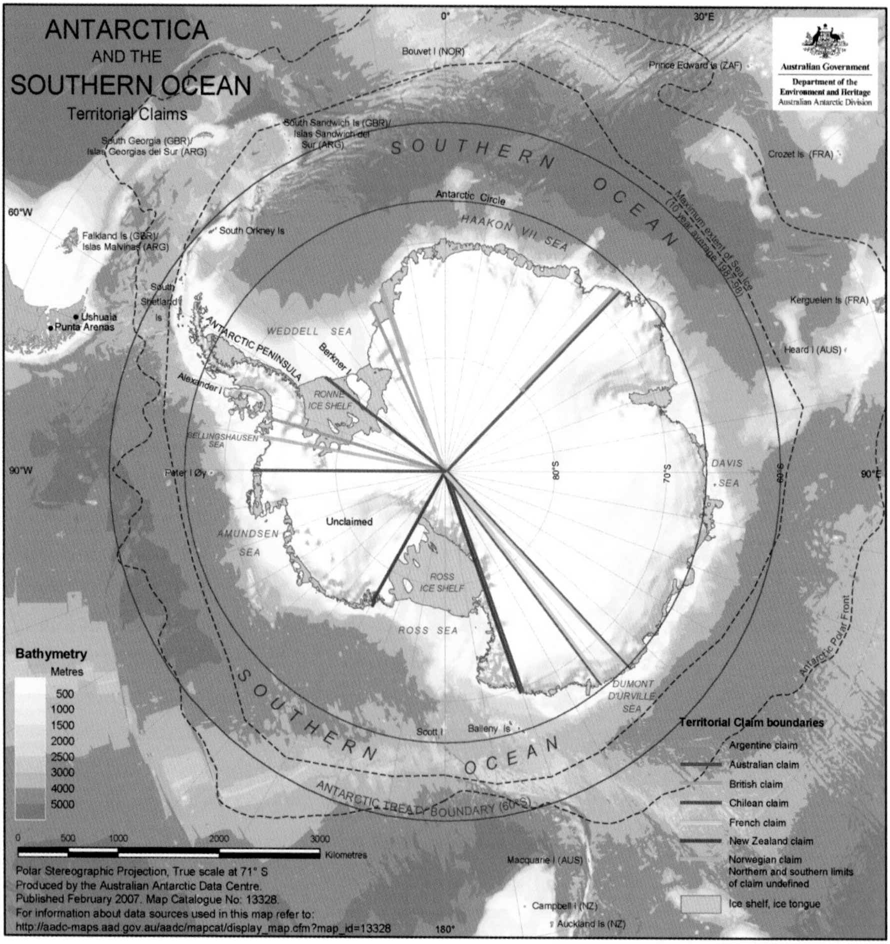
ANTARCTICA
AND THE
SOUTHERN OCEAN
Territorial Claims
Australian Government
Department of the Environment and Heritage
Australian Antarctic Division
0°
30°E
60°W
90°W
90°E
180°
Bouvet I (NOR)
Prince Edward Is (ZAF)
Crozet Is (FRA)
Kerguelen Is (FRA)
Heard I (AUS)
South Georgia (GBR)/
Islas Georgias del Sur (ARG)
South Sandwich Is (GBR)/
Islas Sandwich del Sur (ARG)
Falkland Is (GBR)/
Islas Malvinas (ARG)
South Orkney Is
South Shetland Is
Ushuaia
Punta Arenas
SOUTHERN OCEAN
Antarctic Circle
Maximum extent of Sea Ice (10 year average 1987-98)
HAAKON VII SEA
WEDDELL SEA
ANTARCTIC PENINSULA
Berkner I
Alexander I
RONNE ICE SHELF
BELLINGSHAUSEN SEA
Peter I Øy
Unclaimed
AMUNDSEN SEA
ROSS ICE SHELF
ROSS SEA
DAVIS SEA
80°S
70°S
60°S
DUMONT D'URVILLE SEA
Scott I
Balleny Is
ANTARCTIC TREATY BOUNDARY (60°S)
Antarctic Polar Front
Macquarie I (AUS)
Campbell I (NZ)
Auckland Is (NZ)
Bathymetry
Metres
500
1000
1500
2000
2500
3000
4000
5000
0
500
1000
2000
3000
Kilometres
Territorial Claim boundaries
Argentine claim
Australian claim
British claim
Chilean claim
French claim
New Zealand claim
Norwegian claim
Northern and southern limits of claim undefined
Ice shelf, ice tongue
Polar Stereographic Projection, True scale at 71° S
Produced by the Australian Antarctic Data Centre.
Published February 2007. Map Catalogue No: 13328.
For information about data sources used in this map refer to:
http://aadc-maps.aad.gov.au/aadc/mapcat/display_map.cfm?map_id=13328

Preface

It is hard to think of a stranger place than the South Pole – if you can call it a place at all. Humans have theorized its existence for millennia, but our history of actual encounter with the South Pole is remarkably short – a little over a century. Many people equate it with a whole continent – Antarctica – but the Pole itself is technically just a point. There is no doubt about its cartographic position: 90 degrees south. But try to locate the Pole on a standard map and you may find yourself tracing out a line along its bottom; it does not slot easily into our conventional ways of looking at the world.

In the popular imagination, the South Pole is the most remote point on the globe. However, as one of two points where Earth's rotational axis meets its surface, it is also about as central a place as you can find: the whole planet revolves around it. The topography of the Pole is both remarkable and tedious: it 'sits' atop several miles of ice, on a largely featureless plateau. There is not, on the face of it, a lot to recommend the place: it is dark for half the year; its freezing climate is entirely hostile to all organic life above the level of the microbe; its economic value is minimal; and it is a long way from anywhere. In the early decades of the twentieth century, however, this point on Earth was more sought after than any other. Six nations' territorial claims now meet there, although it remains, like all of Antarctica, unowned.

My aim here is to tell the story of humanity's relationship with the Pole – one that begins in speculation and imagination, moves through exploration and tragedy, becomes rooted in

This map shows the wedge-shaped territorial claims to the Antarctic converging on the South Pole (only the Norwegian claim has an unspecified southern limit).

settlement and science, but remains open to geopolitical machinations. This story pivots around two key historical events, nearly 50 years apart. One is the first arrival of explorers at the Pole: the Norwegian Antarctic Expedition led by Roald Amundsen reached the longed-for point in late 1911. They were followed about a month later by a five-man British party led by Robert Falcon Scott, all of whom died on the return leg, generating a tragic story that has eclipsed Amundsen's success in the public imagination. The other event is the construction of the first scientific station at 90 degrees south by the United States in 1956–7, named 'Amundsen-Scott South Pole Station' in honour of the two expedition leaders. The very existence of a

Ole Larsen jr.

Tidens Tegn

Verktøimaskiner,
Træforædlingsmaskiner.
Shaw-Kuplinger.
Staalremskiver
C. G. RUDE.

Nr. 68. | Utkommer hver morgen. | Kristiania, lørdag 9. mars 1912. | Redigert av O. Thommessen. | 3. aarg.

L. Haak & Co.

P. A. LARSEN'S CALORICPUNSCH. Blaa Etiket.

Amundsens egen beretning om Sydpolsfærden.

Til polen gjennem mægtig fjeldnatur. — Polplataaet bærer Kong Haakons navn.

Telegram til „Tidens Tegn" og „Aftenposten".

Hanna Ebbells Blomsterforretning

Bømmel

Paul Frank

Kr. 1.40 pr. Kilo
Haugesund Smerfabrik

A. F. Jansen's Bokbinderi

Elektroteknisk laboratorium

MEDDELELSE
Dr. Greve's Barnesæbe.

WDM. SCHIOLDBORG

Abonner paa
Tidens Tegn
De hurtigste og beste efterretninger fra ind- og utland.
Av alle landets politiske blade nr. 1 utenbys, nr. 2 indenbys.
Abonnement koster i Kristiania 60 øre maaneden, utenbys kr. 2,25 kvartalet.

A Norwegian newspaper promises readers Amundsen's own narrative of the South Pole expedition, sent by telegram. The Norwegians' arrival at the Pole had been announced from Hobart on 7 March. The photograph of Amundsen is actually a publicity shot taken near his home, not far from Oslo, prior to the expedition.

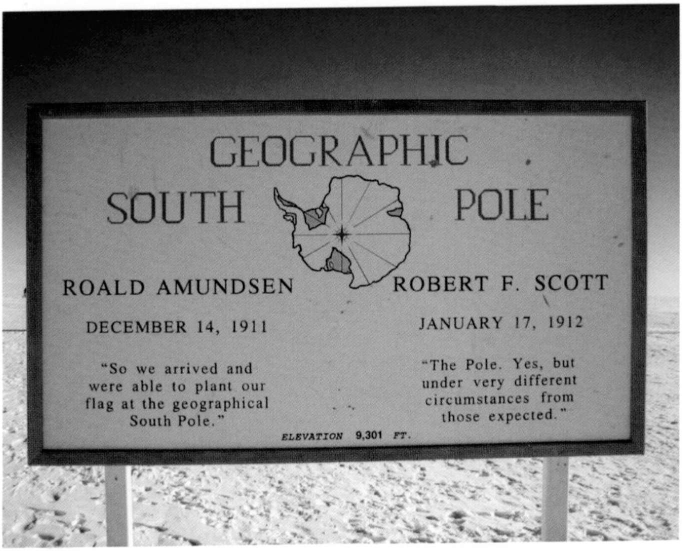

Sign marking the Geographic South Pole.

permanent station points to one of many important differences between the North and South poles. Unlike its northern counterpart, the South Pole is solid. Although it is ice rather than land, it can be built and lived upon, meaning that its history of human interaction has been quite different from that of the Arctic pole.

I also want to complicate the story of the South Pole as it is popularly told. I have been talking here about *the* South Pole, but there are, as I will explain, many 'South Poles', not all of them stationary. While my focus is primarily the Geographic South Pole, from time to time I turn to various 'other' poles. And despite Antarctica being dubbed the 'continent for science', I want to emphasize that the Pole is not just a natural place, a goal for explorers and an important site for scientists. It is also a very political and contested place, as well as a cultural place, one that is continually re-imagined and represented. The South Pole is a real point on the Earth that can be visited – tourists pay a large price to do so – but it is also a highly charged symbol.

At first glance, the Pole might seem an impossible subject for the writer, let alone the artist or photographer. How much is there to say about a remote point on an ice plateau that cannot even be located without complicated observations and calculations? As it turns out, a great deal – much more than can be squeezed into a book of this size. Images and ideas have accreted around the Pole during thousands of years of geographical speculation, and the previous century, with its sledging journeys and overflights, international political negotiations, scientific investigations, infrastructure construction, environmental crises and tourist visits, has added many new meanings and mythologies. This book attempts to weave together these diverse facets of the South Pole.

1 Where is the South Pole?

Where is the South Pole? It seems a nonsensical question. Ninety degrees south: what could be more singular, more precise, than the location of the South Pole?

It was just this question, however, that in late 1911 exercised the first men to reach the Pole's vicinity: the Norwegian Roald Amundsen and his four companions. Faced with a featureless icy waste much like the rest of the plateau they had traversed for weeks, they needed to locate their target as accurately as possible. Despite their initial celebrations, flag-planting and national proclamations, 'every one of us knew that we were not standing on the absolute spot.'[1] The controversy surrounding apparent arrivals at the North Pole a few years previously by Frederick Cook and Robert Peary was a salient lesson. Neither Arctic explorer had proved beyond doubt that he had actually reached his goal, and a heated dispute had ensued.

Amundsen's team, then, did not rest on their laurels. The leader sent three men out on skis, two perpendicular to their original path and one in the same direction, travelling out about 20 km (12.5 miles) and using spare sledge-runners as markers. The task exposed the three skiers to some danger: any one of them could have lost his way (and hence his life) on the blank expanse of the plateau. Meanwhile, the remaining two men took hourly observations of the sun's elevations to determine their position. As a result, they moved 9 km (5.5 miles) further on, planted another flag, set up their spare tent in which they left letters – one for the Norwegian king, one for the British expedition leader Robert F. Scott, then still on his way south – and took now-famous photographs. In a bold attempt at domestication, they named the place 'Polheim', just as they had called their coastal base 'Framheim'. More observations ensued: 'we were not on the absolute Pole, but as close to it as we could hope to get with our instruments'. Skiers were sent out yet again, 'to come a few inches nearer to the actual Pole'.[2]

When Scott's team arrived a month later, their situation was very different: where they had hoped for blankness, they were confronted by the marks of human activity. Making their own measurements, they took an upright sledge-runner they found as the Norwegians' best approximation of the actual Pole. It was about 800 m (half a mile) from the point where the British had held their own more despondent arrival ceremony. The Norwegians, Scott reflected, had 'made thoroughly sure of their mark'.[3] In the end, both teams located the Pole with remarkable accuracy, but it took some doing. The South Pole was not easy to find.

More than 100 years later, the Pole has stayed put (more or less) but, subject to continual ice movement and accumulating

Sculptor Håkon Fagerås created these bronze statues of Amundsen's team outside the Fram Museum in Oslo to mark the centenary of the first arrival at the Pole.

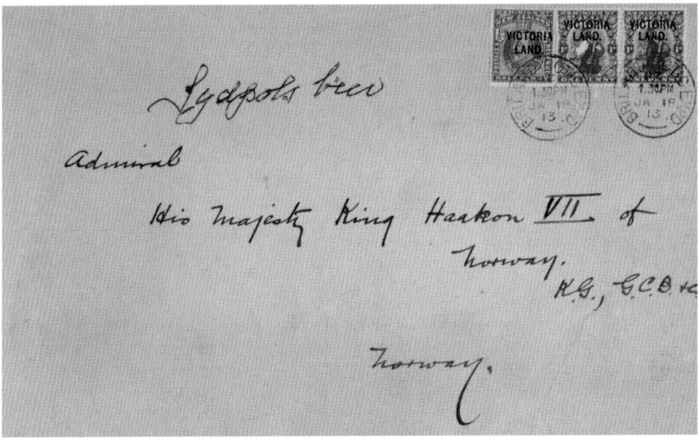

The letter (*bottom right*) Amundsen left at the South Pole for the King of Norway, and the envelope in which it was eventually sent from Britain after it was retrieved from Scott's party.

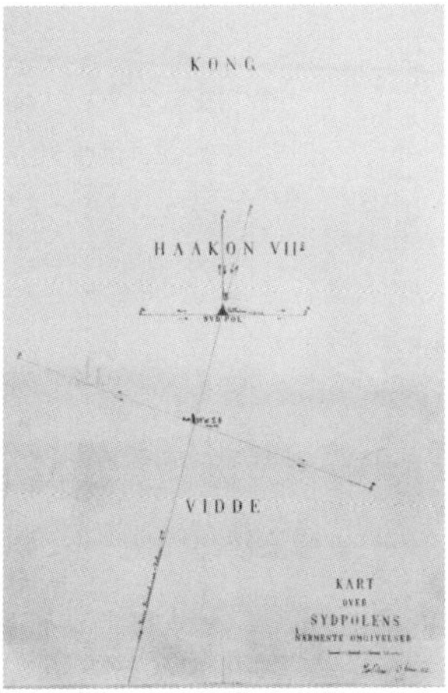

Thorvald Nilsen's map (6 February 1912) of the region near the South Pole traversed by Amundsen's team was reproduced in the expedition narrative *The South Pole*.

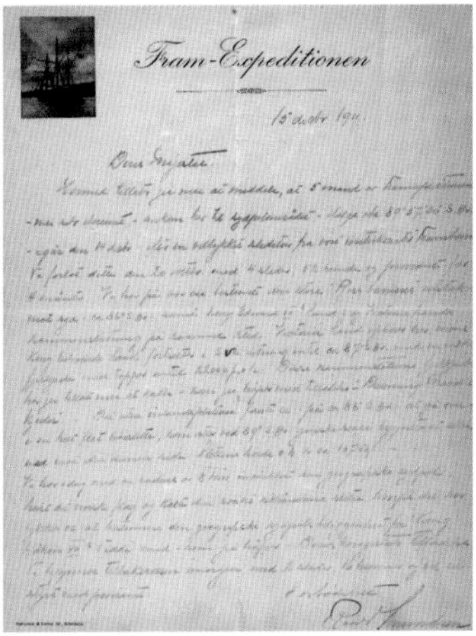
Fram-Expeditionen

15 dcbr 1911

snow, the signs of the first human encounter with this 'last of all places' have moved on – and down. All the artefacts left by Amundsen's team at Polheim – the tent, the letters, the flag, the abandoned equipment and clothes – are now under about 17 m (55 feet) of ice. Ironically, scientific calculations suggest that Amundsen's tent, at a little more than 2 kilometres) from the Pole, may now be slightly closer to the Norwegians' target than it was in 1911.[4]

The Antarctic ice is always shifting, meaning that no marker stays at '90 south' for long. These days two different markers are used. The first is the photogenic Ceremonial Pole: a shiny

Hanssen's photograph of Wisting, Bjaaland, Hassel and Amundsen (and dogs) at the South Pole, 14 December 1911.

Amundsen and Hanssen use a sextant to determine their position. This copy of the photograph, signed by Bjaaland, was presented to South Pole residents in 1961.

SOUTH POLE, DEC 14, 1911.– FROM THE ONLY SURVIVOR IN 1961, OLAV BJAALAND.(See back side)

December 23, 1911]
THE SPHERE
285
Has Captain Scott Reached the Pole To-day?
ROSS SEA
Great Barrier Reef
McMurdo Sound
Mt Terra Nova
Mt Terror
Mt Erebus
Depot
Minna Bluff
Mt Lister
Mt Discovery
Depots laid well to the South by April 1911
Depot
Barne Inlet
LOWER PLATEAU
Shackleton Inlet
Mt Hope
Probable Main Depot. Start for the Pole Oct
Beardmore Glacier (November)
UPPER PLATEAU
SOUTH POLE Dec 22nd ?
DRAWN BY G. BRUN
A "DOWN-UNDER" VIEW OF CAPTAIN SCOTT'S ROUTE TO THE SOUTH POLE
Captain Robert Falcon Scott with his gallant men hoped to reach the South Pole to-day (Friday, December 22) if everything went well. We hope all has gone well. This view shows the South-Polar region lit with the sunshine of the daylight period as it would really appear when viewed from space in relation to ourselves. On the opposite page are given the chief dates of Captain Scott's programme.

British magazine *The Sphere* provides readers with a 'down-under view' of Scott's route in late December 1911.

spherical mirror on a red-and-white barbershop-style column, surrounded by a semicircle of flags representing the twelve nations that originally signed the Antarctic Treaty of 1959. This serves for obligatory 'hero shots' and official occasions, but is a few hundred metres away from the Geographic Pole. The second, less permanent marker is a metal post (a pole, if you like) indicating the actual site of 90 degrees south, accompanied by a

A famous 'selfie': Bowers took this photograph of Scott's party at the South Pole using a string attached to the camera. L–R: Oates, Bowers, Scott, Wilson, Evans.

sign and an American flag, and surmounted by an ornamental metal disc. It moves with the ice about 10 m (30 feet) every year, so is annually replaced by a new marker (carefully designed by South Pole Station personnel), in the corrected position, during a ceremony held on New Year's Day.[5] The sites of the old Pole positions are marked by stakes, the line of them indicating the movement of the ice.

Just as the ice is constantly shifting, so is the continent itself, although on a much longer timescale. The South Pole has not always been in Antarctica – or rather, Antarctica has not always been at the South Pole. Five hundred million years ago, the continent probably lay on or near the equator, butting against Australia, India, Africa and South America as part of the supercontinent of Gondwana. At points in this long history the South Pole was covered by ocean rather than land. Antarctica wandered around the high southern latitudes, but only in the last 35 million years, after it had drifted towards the Pole and broken from Australia and South America, did it begin to take on its present icy form.[6]

Antarctica's isolation means that the South Pole is physically quite different from the North. The ancient Greeks' coinage of the adjective *Ant-arktikos* – meaning, essentially, opposite the north (Arktos, 'the bear', is a northern constellation) – was accurate in more than just an astronomic or geographic sense. The South Pole sits on more than 2,700 m (9,000 feet) of ice, under which is the bedrock of a continent, itself surrounded by a large uninterrupted body of water – the Southern Ocean. The North Pole by contrast sits on sea ice only a few metres thick, in the middle of the Arctic Ocean, which is surrounded by land. There are, of course, also physical similarities. Both places are very cold, due to the low angle at which the sun's rays hit them and the reflection of sunlight by the white ice. The South Pole, however, positioned high up in the interior of a continent, is far colder. The Earth's tilting axis is also responsible for the diurnal extremes at each Pole: a 'day' famously lasts half the year, with sunrise at the South Pole occurring in September, at the spring equinox, and sunset at the autumnal equinox in March, six months later. Weeks of twilight separate the long periods of light and dark.

The issue of the Earth's rotation brings a new complication to the question 'Where is the South Pole?' A marker placed on the South Pole might move due to the shifting of the ice underneath, and the continent on which the Pole 'sits' might in the far future drift away from under it again, but the Pole itself – defined as the place where the planet's axis of spin meets its surface – might be expected intuitively to remain stationary relative to the

2012 Geographic South Pole marker.

planet itself. But this is not the case. The reason is the shape of Earth. Although we like to think of our planet as a perfect sphere, it is a rather messier body, a little squashed at the top and bottom (giving it an 'oblate spheroid' shape) and slightly asymmetrical. It is this asymmetry, as well as periodic changes in the distribution of its mass (such as the seasonal displacement of air and water and changes in the fluid mantle), that makes the Earth's axis of rotation move relative to the planet's surface, in a roughly spiral motion. This 'polar motion' would not have been significant enough to upset Amundsen or Scott – it never causes either pole to vary more than a matter of metres from an average position. In addition to this roughly periodic shift, however, the poles are undergoing a slow irregular drift. This drift is due to non-periodic movements of the Earth's own matter – shifting water masses as well as changes within the planet's interior. The North Pole has been meandering southwards over the last 100 years, travelling on average along the 70 degrees west meridian (the direction of Canada).[7] The South Pole is taking its own path – presumably the opposite of the North's.[8] Again, the change is minute on a global scale – about 0.1 m (4 inches) per year at the North Pole since the turn of the twentieth century.[9]

All this assumes that, when the question 'Where is the South Pole?' is asked, we are all talking about the same South Pole. In the above, I have used 'South Pole' as shorthand for the Geographic South Pole of the Earth (also called the Geographical South Pole or Terrestrial South Pole), and will continue to do so throughout this book, unless otherwise specified. But there are many alternative South Poles, including the Magnetic South Pole, Geomagnetic South Pole, Celestial South Pole and South Pole of Inaccessibility – a veritable polar zoo. Confusingly, these terms are not always used consistently, but vary with context and purpose. Many sources define the Geographic Pole as the point where Earth's rotational axis meets its surface. Others use a different phrase, such as 'pole of rotation' or 'spin pole', to describe this continually shifting point, defining the geographic poles in terms of the Earth's system of cartographic coordinates, as the fixed points where the lines of longitude meet: 90 degrees north and south. As the distance between the pole of rotation and the 'cartographic' pole – 90 degrees south – is so small on a global scale, the distinction makes very little difference to non-technical discussions of the South Pole.

The 'original' South Pole could be found in the heavens rather than on Earth. The term 'Pole' comes from the ancient Greek word *polos* (πόλος) – pivot or axis – which in turn derives from an earlier Indo-European root word meaning 'to be in motion'. While the Presocratic Greeks believed the Earth to be flat, they nonetheless had a concept of a Celestial North Pole: observing that the stars appeared to rotate around the sky from east to west each night, they postulated the existence of a spinning celestial hemisphere and used *polos* to refer to the axis around which it appeared to turn, as well as the end point of this axis. When the Earth was considered to be flat, neither the idea of a southern celestial pole nor the concept of an earthly axis (and hence terrestrial poles) was necessary. When the celestial vault began to be conceived as a sphere rather than a hemisphere (for example, by Anaxagoras in the fifth century BC), however, the

Star trails over the Yepun telescope in Chile circle the Celestial South Pole.

concept of a southern as well as a northern celestial pole became theoretically possible. With the argument for a spherical Earth, consolidated by Aristotle in the fourth century BC, came the necessity for terrestrial poles – points where the celestial axis met the surface of the planet (which was not itself thought to turn). Aristotle's *On the Heavens* mentions the invisible southern celestial pole as well as the visible northern one, and his *Meteorologica* refers to the 'other' pole in a terrestrial context – probably the earliest written reference to the Geographic South Pole.[10] Later Greek and Roman thinkers such as Eratosthenes, Cicero, Pliny the Elder, Strabo and Ptolemy refer, either implicitly or directly, to the southern as well as the northern terrestrial pole. Many thinkers of the Middle Ages also assumed a spherical model of the Earth and hence the existence of a southern terrestrial pole.[11] Geoffrey Chaucer's *Treatise on the Astrolabe* (1391) includes one of the earliest written references to the concept in English.

The celestial poles remain useful theoretical concepts today, referring to the points where the Earth's axis of rotation, extended out arbitrarily far, meets an imaginary sphere on which the distant stars appear to sit. If you are standing at either of the geographic poles, the corresponding celestial pole should be directly above your head, staying still as the rest of the stars seem to circle around it. However, on a long timescale this point also changes position relative to the stars: the Earth's axis of rotation precesses – it wobbles like a top – causing the Celestial South Pole to move in a circle over a period of nearly 26,000 years. This phenomenon (distinct from the polar motion described earlier) is caused by the Earth's 'squashed sphere' shape and the gravitational pull of other bodies in the solar system.

At present, the Celestial North Pole is located within the constellation of the Little Bear (Ursa Minor). The constellation's brightest star, once known as Cynosura, is now called Polaris, the Pole Star (or 'lodestar'). It has not always been the Pole Star, however: the Celestial Pole moves away from and towards different stars during its 26,000-year cycle. Since late antiquity, Polaris has been close enough to the Celestial North Pole to act as a beacon for navigators, and has been moving ever closer in the

Earth's tilted axis of rotation is responsible for the diurnal extremes in the polar regions. The axis 'points' in either direction towards the celestial poles.

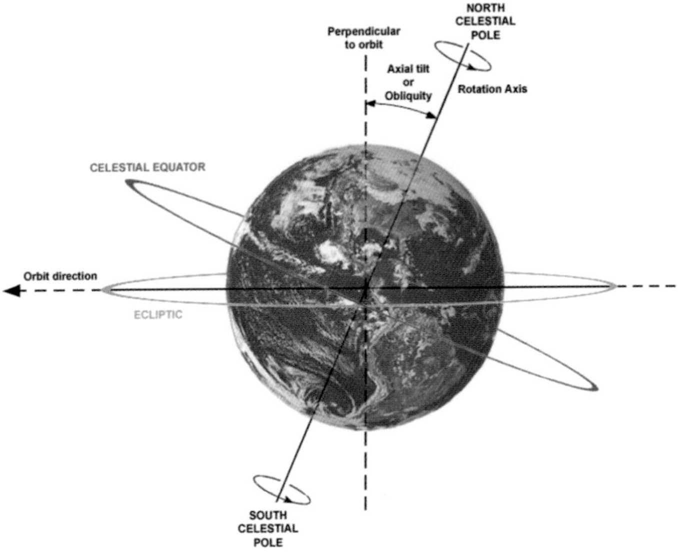

period since. It will reach its nearest point around AD 2100, after which its distance from the Celestial Pole will start to increase, and eventually another star will take on its role. The Celestial South Pole has no conveniently bright stellar guide of this kind to mark its whereabouts: it has to make do with a dim constellation, and its designated pole star – Sigma Octantis or Polaris Australis – is not easy to see even when the weather is clear.

Most commonly confused with the geographic poles are the magnetic poles: the two points where the Earth's magnetic field lines are perpendicular to its surface. A compass needle that is free to move vertically should point directly down at the Magnetic North Pole and up at the South; the magnetic poles are correspondingly referred to as the 'dip' poles. The existence of these planetary magnetic poles was first postulated to explain the behaviour of magnetic materials. Early forms of the compass were employed by the Chinese by the first century AD and by the twelfth century they had entered into usage by Europeans. There were various speculations about why the lodestones used in these compasses aligned themselves along a north–south line, including a postulated enormous lodestone at the Geographical North Pole or special properties of the Pole Star itself. A French scholar known as Petrus Peregrinus ('the wanderer') in the later thirteenth century first noticed the polarity of the lodestone, likening its two poles to the celestial northern and southern poles of the cosmos.[12]

At this stage the north indicated by the stars (what has since been called 'true north') and the north indicated by a compass ('magnetic north') were thought to be one and the same. In fact, in most locations, a compass needle deviates from the direction of the North Geographic Pole by a significant angle, meaning that there is a considerable distance between true and magnetic north; the same goes for the south. However, this phenomenon, known as 'declination', was recognized only slowly over the next few centuries. The concept that the Earth has its own magnetic field – that it is itself, in effect, a giant magnet – was first suggested in 1600 by William Gilbert, physician to Elizabeth I. In Gilbert's model the Earth's magnetic and rotational axes are aligned, putting the magnetic and geographic poles in the same place. Gilbert knew about declination but explained it by suggesting that the magnetism of rocks in the continents caused local deviations of the compass needle. Just a few years later his idea was modified, so that the magnetic axis was now tilted away from the rotational one, placing the magnetic poles well apart from their geographic counterparts, although still in high latitudes. The theory – which essentially postulates an enormous tilted bar magnet (a magnetic 'dipole') sitting at the planet's centre – did not, however, explain observations particularly well. The patterns of declination were far too complex to fit this simple model.[13]

To make matters more complex, it was increasingly recognized that declination – and hence the relative position of the geographic and magnetic poles – varied over time. This suggested that the magnetic poles, like Petrus Peregrinus, were wanderers. Scientists continued to suggest explanations: Edmond Halley (of comet fame) in the late seventeenth century postulated the existence of four magnetic poles – one pair in the north, the other in the south. Halley speculated that the Earth contained within itself another sphere: two of the magnetic poles were produced by the outer sphere of the Earth and two by his speculative inner sphere. The two spheres rotated at different speeds, in Halley's model, explaining the way that the deviation of the compass needle from true north varied over time. There could, he suggested, be a series of nested shells inside the Earth; he even raised the possibility of the planet's interior being inhabited.[14]

As understandings of both magnetism and the Earth's interior progressed over the following three centuries, increasingly precise theories were developed. The tilted, centred bar-magnet model is now understood as a very roughly approximate version of the actual situation. The term 'geomagnetic pole' is applied to the two points, north and south, where the field lines of this imaginary bar magnet would be perpendicular to the Earth's surface. In actuality, however, the Earth's magnetic field is a dynamic system with some components that act like big bar magnets and others that do not ('dipole' and 'non-dipole'). The movement of molten metal within Earth's mantle accounts for the wandering of the magnetic poles, and the influence of electrically charged particles from the sun produces an additional daily, roughly elliptical motion. These particles also create auroral effects (the northern and southern 'lights'). There are, however, only two magnetic poles – points where the Earth's magnetic field is perpendicular to its surface – which are the net product of this complex system. Unlike the geomagnetic poles, the northern and southern magnetic poles are not directly opposite each other, nor do they move at the same rate.

For nineteenth-century scientists and navigators, a practical question remained: where on Earth are the magnetic poles? What are their coordinates of latitude and longitude? Unsurprisingly, the Magnetic North Pole was the first point of focus: British naval expeditions searching for the Northwest Passage also took detailed magnetic observations. In 1831 John Ross captained an expedition during which a small party led by his nephew James Clark Ross finally reached the spot. Like Amundsen, Ross knew he was not technically on the precise Pole, but rather very close to it: 'if popular conversation', he later wrote, 'gives to this voyage the credit of having placed its flag on the very point, on the summit of that mysterious pole which it perhaps views as a visible and tangible reality, it can now correct itself as it may please'.[15] Neither was he necessarily the first person to reach its immediate vicinity, since he took his observations from conveniently located abandoned Inuit huts. Nonetheless, he was justifiably happy with his scientific achievement and, fewer than ten years later, he was leading an expedition in the Antarctic that hoped to reach the Magnetic South Pole.

This task was close to impossible at the time, as Ross discovered when he fixed the Pole's location: his goal was within the Antarctic continent, unreachable by ship. When its attainment was eventually announced about 70 years later, problems with the accuracy of its location still occurred: a team, including the Australian explorer and scientist Douglas Mawson, thought they had reached the Magnetic South Pole in early 1909, only to discover years later, after their figures had been analysed by experts, that technically they hadn't. The Magnetic South Pole can now be found in the ocean off the Antarctic coast, around 1,400 km (900 miles) from its position in Ross's time, and nearly 2,900 km (1,800 miles) from the Geographic South Pole.[16] It is currently drifting northwest (towards Australia) at about 10–15 km (6–9 miles) per year – a sluggish rate compared to its northern cousin, which has been moving in a similar direction (from Canada towards Siberia) at up to 60 km (37 miles) per year.[17]

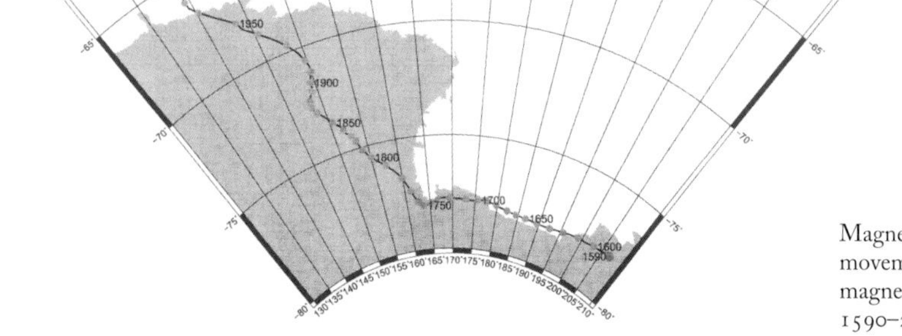

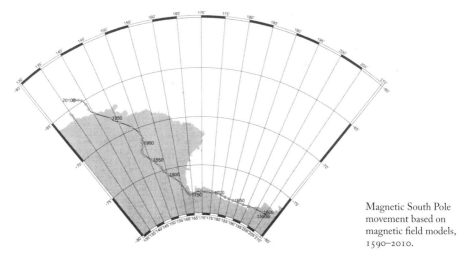

Magnetic South Pole movement based on magnetic field models, 1590–2010.

Ironically the Magnetic North Pole is technically a south pole of the Earth's magnetic field, and vice versa. Historically, the north pole of a magnet was the end that pointed north; but, because opposite poles attract, it was a *south* magnetic pole in the Arctic pulling the compass needle's north end. However, this has not always been the case: over geological timescales, the polarity of the Earth's geomagnetic field can shift, so that 800,000 years ago the Magnetic South Pole would indeed have been a magnetic south pole. While the process of this 'flip' is occurring – it can take up to 10,000 years – the geomagnetic system is in a disordered state, and at times there may be more than one north and south magnetic pole. Many such reversals have occurred in Earth's geological history.

There is yet another South Pole to be canvassed – a pole by name more than nature. A 'pole of inaccessibility' is the term applied to a place that is the most difficult of its kind to reach. In continents this is conventionally taken as the point furthest from the coast, on average; in oceans it is the furthest point from the surrounding lands. The South Pole of Inaccessibility (sometimes qualified as 'Relative Inaccessibility' or 'Maximum Inaccessibility') is thus the point in Antarctica that is on average furthest from the continent's coast. Since locating the coastline has not itself always been straightforward, and depends on whether ice shelves are included, it is possible to find several different estimates of its location; 85°S, 65°E is commonly cited these days. The Geographic South Pole is not, as is sometimes assumed, in the centre of the continent – even roughly. It lies many hundreds of miles from the Pole of Inaccessibility, however the latter is estimated.

The 'pole of cold' is another term that uses 'pole' synonymously with 'extreme'. It refers either to the point in a continent with the coldest mean annual temperature or the point with the lowest individual recorded temperature. Antarctica can boast the coldest pole of cold in both interpretations: the lowest recorded air temperature in the world –89.2°C (–128.6°F) occurred at the Russian base Vostok; mean temperatures are slightly colder at Dome A, which is also the region of highest altitude in the

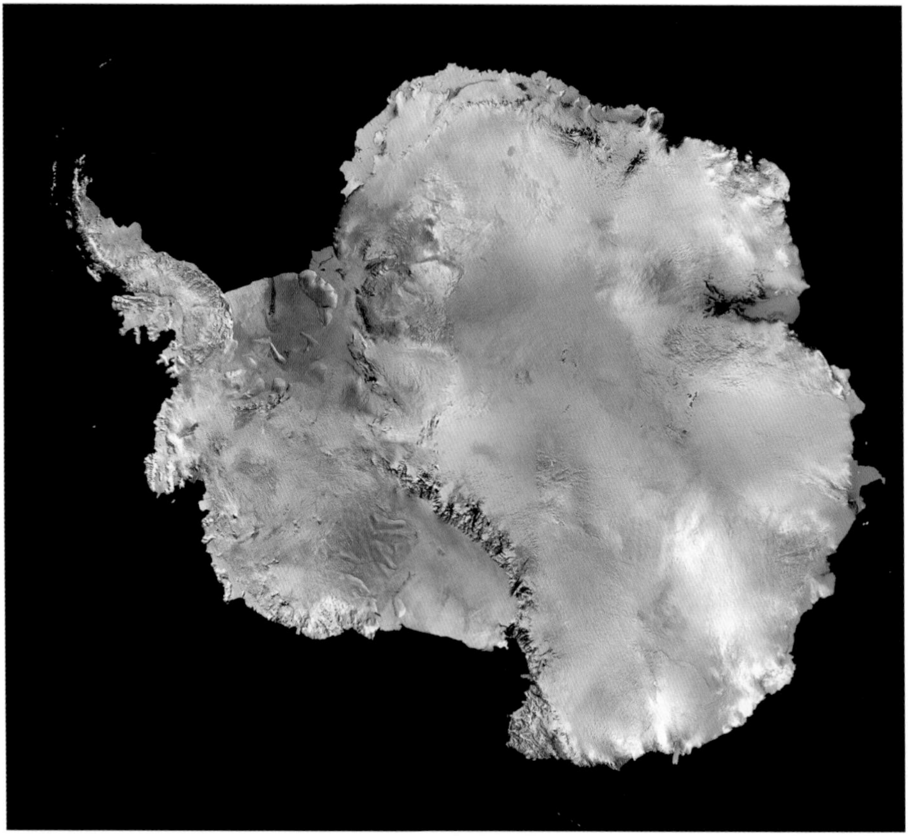

Satellite image of Antarctica generated from NASA's Visible Earth Blue Marble project.

continent at just over 4 km (2.5 miles). Both are significantly colder than the lower Geographic South Pole.

Just one South Pole remains: Antarctica itself. Anyone picking up this book could be forgiven for assuming that its subject is the south polar region, broadly speaking – the whole Antarctic continent and its surrounding seas. 'I write to enquire whether you will do me the favour – and honour – of joining my expedition to the South Pole': so runs a letter from Mawson to a potential expedition member,[18] but the Australian explorer had no intention of going to the Geographic Pole, and had in fact refused an invitation from Scott to do so. He planned to (and did) base his expedition on the coast of East Antarctica, barely within the Antarctic Circle, half a continent away from

Scott's destination. In his letter, however, Mawson uses 'South Pole' and 'Antarctica' interchangeably, as many people still do.[19]

Inasmuch as my subject of interest lies within the southernmost continent, this *is* a book about Antarctica. But my main focus is that strange point in Antarctica's interior – a point that is symbolically the most remote of earthly locations and simultaneously a centre to which explorers, adventurers, scientists and now even tourists are inexorably drawn. Despite the evident absurdity of making an expensive and (for those who still choose to travel overland) arduous journey to an extremely inhospitable point on a comparatively featureless ice plateau, the lure remains. There is something remarkable in standing at (to borrow T. S. Eliot's phrase) a 'still point of the turning world':

> Except for the point, the still point,
> There would be no dance, and there is only the dance.
> I can only say, *there* we have been: but I cannot say where.[20]

2 Maps and Mythologies

Open any standard atlas and the first map of the world that you see will almost certainly place the equatorial region near its centre, the Arctic at the top and the Antarctic at the bottom. The equator itself is rarely in the exact middle of the map; more often it is someway down the bottom half of the page, so that the lion's share of space is given to the northern hemisphere, and the Antarctic coast pokes out from the lower edge of the frame, if it is there at all. One researcher, flying with the Australian airline Qantas in the early twenty-first century, was taken aback to find that the map provided in the in-flight magazine, despite giving considerable detail about remote regions where the airline does not fly (such as Arctic islands), overlooked the entire continent to Australia's south, although its aircraft are regularly chartered for flights over the region.[1] In many common cartographical projections the Antarctic (and Arctic) are distorted more than other regions. In the Mercator projection the poles become horizontal lines, impossibly smeared out along the borders of the map. When it does appear, then, the 'other Pole' is often treated to the double indignity of being grossly attenuated and 'at the bottom'.

The South Pole has not always been the underdog. In *On the Heavens* Aristotle refers to the invisible southern celestial pole as 'the one on top' (although in his *Meteorologica* it is the north that has this position).[2] Chinese compasses were originally oriented to the south rather than the north.[3] Early Arabic maps tended to be south-oriented, and influenced maps produced in Italy.

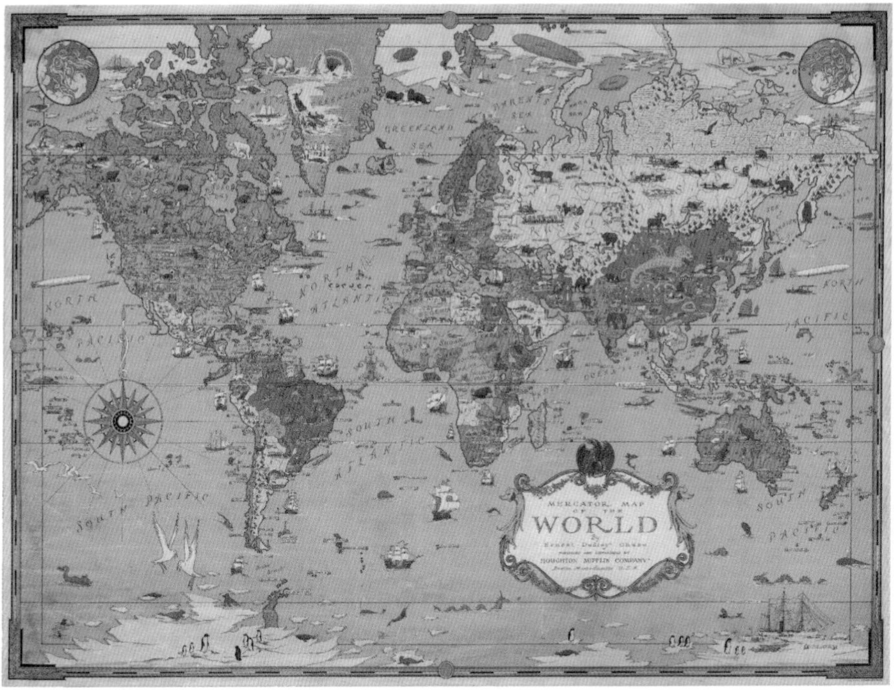

A 1931 pictorial map of the world using the Mercator projection.

Medieval *mappaemundi*, most of which are constrained to the known parts of the world and so do not include the space where Antarctica would be, normally have the East, the site of Jerusalem, at the top, although some, including one of the most famous, by Fra Mauro, are south-oriented.[4]

As Western cartography began to burgeon alongside exploration and trade during the Renaissance, however, the main influence was Ptolemy's *Geographia*, a treatise from the second century AD which had only recently been revived in Europe; and Ptolemy placed the north at the top of the map. Drawing on earlier assumptions that a large southern hemisphere landmass must exist to balance the known lands of the north symmetrically, he also posited an enormous continent that he termed *Terra Incognita*, joined to Africa and India and enclosing the Indian Ocean to the south. Another influential figure was the fifth-century AD Roman philosopher Macrobius, whose 'zonal' or 'climatic' world map was reproduced in numerous medieval manuscripts (sometimes with a south orientation). Following a theory that reached back many centuries to the Greek philosopher Parmenides, Macrobius divided the world into five climatic zones, with the far north and south both frigid, the equatorial region torrid and the two zones in-between temperate. Maps based on Macrobius' ideas show a large, cold, southern continent separated from northern lands by an ocean.

From the fifteenth century to the eighteenth, representations of the south polar region on European maps are characterized by several contrasting traditions, sometimes incorporating and sometimes ignoring the accumulating but fragmentary information coming back from sea voyages into comparatively high southern latitudes. One line of cartographical speculation was that the far south was simply ocean; another that it was a sea of ice which covered the Pole, with a large island nearby. A third school of thought proposed a ring-shaped continent surrounding a polar sea, and a fourth – the most enduring – maintained a belief in Ptolemy's *Terra Incognita*.[5] On some maps, the southern continent was enormous in extent, extending up as far as New Guinea. An early example of the tradition is Oronce Finé's world map of 1531, drawn using a double cordiform (heart-shaped) projection that foregrounds the polar regions: its *Terra Australis* (this was the first use of the term on a map) is confidently described (in

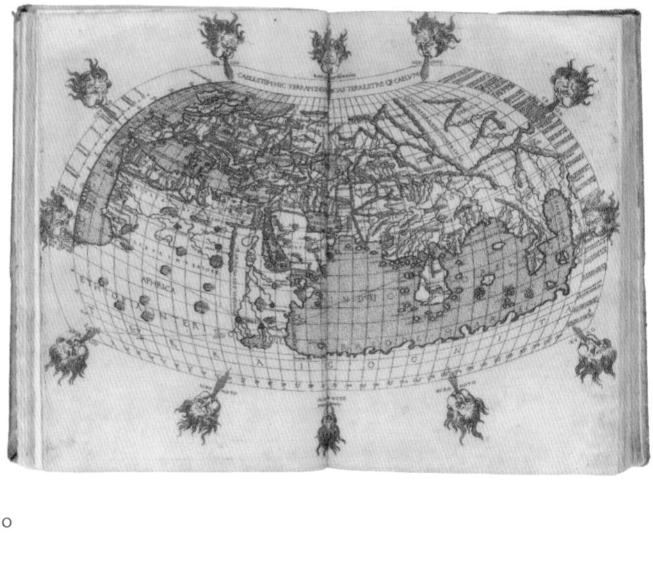

This world map from Francesco Berlinghieri's edition of Ptolemy's *Geographia* (1482) shows a sprawling *Terra Incognita* and a landlocked Indian Ocean.

World map after Macrobius, 1492.

Latin) as 'recently discovered but not yet fully known'.[6] The continent reaches from the Pole up to Tierra del Fuego, which is the land 'recently discovered' (by Magellan), and is nine times larger than the Antarctica known today.[7]

While some maps featuring a large southern continent leave it essentially bare or seize on the extra space to add text and illustrations related to the map as a whole, others fill the unknown area with speculative topography, flora, fauna and human inhabitants. One late sixteenth-century Flemish polar projection has mountains and trees near the Pole.[8] Another Flemish cartographer of the same period, a Jesuit missionary living in China, put a blue giraffe in high southern latitudes, with the Pole occupied with what looks like a crocodile.[9] An Italian world map from around 1530 shows a continent ringing the Pole at a latitude higher than the Antarctic Circle, featuring 'a profusion of named rivers, capes, cities and ports'.[10] On other maps an otherwise empty Pole is marked by a cherub conventionally personifying the south wind, 'Auster'. The place itself is given the name 'Polus Antarcticus' or 'Meridies'. The latter was a term used to signify the 'furthest known point south', deriving from the Latin *medidies*, or midday – the point when, in the northern hemisphere, the sun is due south.[11]

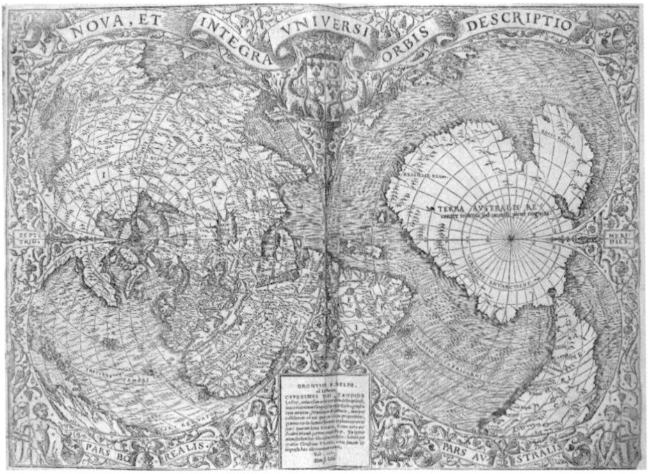

Oronce Finé's double cordiform map of 1531 showing the polar regions.

European maps were not, of course, the only way of expressing an awareness of or speculation about Antarctica and the South Pole. The northern and southern terrestrial poles are described in ancient Indian epics, and the sixth-century Indian astronomer Aryabhata argued that 'the South Pole was surrounded by oceans . . . while the North Pole was surrounded by a landmass'.[12] The famous map produced in 1513 by the Turkish cartographer Piri Reis and rediscovered in 1929 generated excited speculation that the coastline of its southernmost landmass accurately depicted the outline of the Antarctic continent in a much earlier, ice-free state. Explanations involving extraterrestrials or ancient civilizations (both of which feature prominently in twentieth-century Antarctic mythology) inevitably followed. The cartographic historian Gregory McIntosh argues convincingly that Reis's landmass is simply part of the tradition of a southern *Terra Incognita* and bears only a superficial resemblance to the Antarctic continent.[13]

Indigenous people living in the far south could actually *see* the celestial pole that the ancient Greeks hypothesized, although they lacked the conveniently bright Pole Star visible in the north from late antiquity. While Aboriginal Australians may not, prior to European contact, have identified the Pole itself, the Aranda and Luritja tribes of central Australia recognized that 'stars within a certain distance from the south celestial pole never fall below the horizon'.[14] People living in the far south of South America passed down mythological narratives that described a permanently frozen southern region.[15] Often cited in Antarctic exploration histories is the Rarotongan legend of Ui-te-rangiora, a seventh-century navigator who sailed south, encountering a foggy, frozen, berg-strewn environment. Ui-te-rangiora may have met icebergs at the latitude of Aotearoa/New Zealand, although the account does suggest an awareness (possibly influenced by European encounter) of frozen regions to the south. Another oral tradition tells of the Polynesian explorer Tamarereti who went south to investigate auroral phenomena: according to the researcher Turi McFarlane, it is 'universally accepted in the Maori world that upon return Reti's canoe . . . brought back with it certain understanding of the physicality of the Antarctic region'.[16]

European mythology of the poles is likewise intertwined with maritime legend, drawn largely from the north and only later applied, through the logic of symmetry or opposition, to the south. When the sixteenth-century Swedish writer Olaus Magnus advised sailors to use wooden, not iron, pegs when building their vessels, he was following a speculation found as far back as Ptolemy: that the North Pole was surmounted by a magnetic mountain (the distinction between geographic and magnetic poles was still developing at this time).[17] More than three centuries later the novelist Jules Verne wrote an Antarctic narrative, *Les sphinx des glaces* (The Sphinx of the Ice Fields, 1897), in which the climax was the revelation of a huge magnetic rock near the South Pole. Unsuspecting sailors could be pulled towards the Pole not just by a massive magnet but also a huge whirlpool. The legend of a North Polar whirlpool can be traced to the lost fourteenth-century manuscript *Inventio fortunata*, whose author may well have drawn on Norse mythology.[18] Like the magnetic mountain, this feature can be found on some Renaissance maps. One early seventeenth-century Italian cartographer, probably expanding on an idea expressed by Plato, describes water flowing into the Earth at both poles.[19] Later in the same century, the Jesuit Athanasius

Kircher in his *Mundus subterraneus* put forward a theory that the globe acted like a human body, with the waters sucked in at the Arctic, passing through the Earth where anything useful is extracted, with the remaining waste being ejected at the South Pole.

There was, it seems, a pressing need for the poles to be marked by something spectacular, whether mountains or whirlpools. Although the British explorer James Clark Ross, reaching the vicinity of the Magnetic North Pole in 1831, knew what to expect, it still seemed somehow surprising that the site was so unremarkable:

> We could have wished that a place so important had possessed more of mark or note. It was scarcely censurable to regret that there was not a mountain to indicate a spot to which so much of interest must ever be attached; and I could even have pardoned any one among us who had been so romantic or absurd as to expect that the magnetic pole was an object as conspicuous and mysterious as the fabled mountain of Sinbad, that it even was a mountain of iron, or a magnet as large as Mont Blanc. But Nature had here erected no monument to denote the spot which she had chosen as the centre of one of her great and dark powers . . .[20]

The same held true in the south: novelists over the centuries have been eager to mark the South Pole. They have adorned it with vortices and giant lodestones, but also more unusual features, natural and artificial: an ice mountain, a magnificent fountain, the town hall of a polar city, a sea channel to a sister Earth, a cosmic channel to the planet Mars.

The most enduring myth, a variation on the whirlpool legend, was a polar hole leading to an interior, perhaps inhabited, Earth. While speculations on the Earth's hollowness were long-standing (Edmond Halley's contribution is mentioned in the previous chapter), the idea grew significantly in popularity – and notoriety – through the energetic campaigning of the retired U.S. Army captain John Cleves Symmes Jr. In a series of pamphlets starting from 1818, Symmes developed and promoted his model of a habitable inner Earth accessible via holes thousands of miles across at both poles, each surrounded by a ring of ice. His South Pole, then, was like an icy version of the southern ring continent, with an enormous hole in its centre. While most people were understandably sceptical, Symmes nonetheless had his advocates; furthermore, the idea gave new impetus to the vortex myth and raised imaginative possibilities that were exploited by novelists throughout the following centuries, most prominently Edgar Allan Poe.

While many polar legends relate to both poles, the dominant convention of north as 'up' had more than just cartographical implications. Describing the celestial poles in his *Georgics*, the ancient Roman poet Virgil writes: 'One pole is always high above us, while the other deep below our feet sees dark Styx and the spirits of the dead.'[21] Indian cosmography attached similarly negative resonances to the South Pole. Ancient Hindu texts established a disc-shaped model of the cosmos, with the sacred mountain Meru at its centre. When this model was transferred to a globe, Mount Meru was placed at the North Pole; the South Polar region was labelled *Sumeruvadavānala,* with 'Sumeru' an

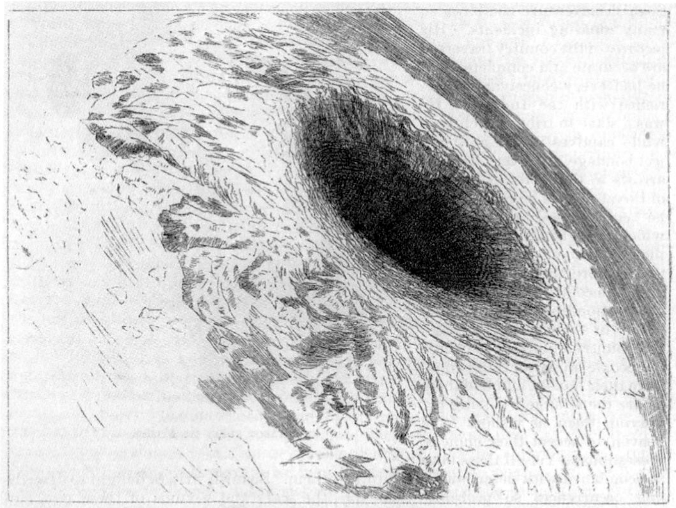

This illustration appeared in an article about Symmes's theory published in *Harper's New Monthly Magazine* in October 1882.

'alternate form of Meru, the axis that penetrates the earth from pole to pole', and *vadavānala* signifying 'a subterranean fire that issues forth from a cavity under the south pole'.[22] Aryabhata, who had access to early globes, believed the South Pole to be 'akin to hell'.[23] Kircher's model of the Earth, with the North Pole as the 'mouth' of the planetary body and the South as its opposite, is similarly hierarchical, putting the latter 'in a most undignified position', to use Joscelyn Godwin's phrase. Godwin, a scholar of occult history, goes on to summarize this polar polarity:

> The mythology surrounding the North Pole has tended to be positive: it is always the Arctic that is imagined as the location of the endless springtime and the cradle of noble races. The Antarctic, on the other hand, is negative: it evokes tales of gloom and destruction, and is populated by primordial horrors, or else by their recent representatives, the Nazis.[24]

Where Kircher likens the poles to bodily orifices, another tradition views them as portals into the self. The contemporary writer Victoria Nelson notes a 'long-standing human tendency to see inner psychological contents – images of wholeness, and ultimately of the self – reflected back from the larger physical contours of our planet'. The poles become 'the orienting loci of the psyche, but by the same token they are also the least known, the farthest from consciousness', with the South Pole the more remote of the two. The narrative pattern of the southern journey is then 'an archetypal sea trip from a bustling port (consciousness) to Terra Australia Incognita (unconsciousness), where a transcendental encounter takes place that initiates either the integration of the self or the possibility of psychic (and physical) annihilation'.[25]

The conflation between psyche and South Pole – and the possibility of madness inherent in this nexus – is given visual expression in a scene from John Carpenter's classic Antarctic horror film, *The Thing* (1982).[26] Set in a remote inland American station at the onset of winter, the film follows the growing paranoia and claustrophobia of a small group of expeditioners as

Still from *The Thing*. Dir. John Carpenter (1982), Universal Pictures.

they deal with an alien being that, having entered the camp in the innocuous form of a sledge dog, attacks and exactly impersonates them one by one. The radio operator, nicknamed 'Windows', is unable to deal with the uncertainty of who is what. He frantically arms himself against the others and has to be talked down at gunpoint by the commander. Eventually, in an attempt to determine who is human and who is alien, the men devise a blood test. The second man to be tested, Windows backs towards the wall as he waits for his result, looking up with worried, glowering eyes. Pinned up behind him on the wall, its outline framing his head, is a map of the Antarctic: it is as if the continent, as much as the Thing, may have somehow got inside him.

The same joining of continent and (un)consciousness is given more positive visual expression in the art of the Canadian Philippe Boissonnet, who travelled to Antarctica with the Argentinian national programme in 2007. Images from his series *The Disenchantment of the World (Atlas)*, part of his installation *This Strange Lightness of the World*, exhibited in Buenos Aires in 2008, play on the nexus between cartography and psychology: one shows a bald man with a south polar projection map drawn onto his cranium. Another shows a mirror image of the man, so that his body blurs into itself, the Arctic on one bald head, the Antarctic on another – a postmodern version of Finé's cordiform world map.

overleaf: Philippe Boissonnet, *In-Between (Atlas' Rescuing)*, ink-jet printing on artist canvas, edition of 3/3, 2008.

Antarctic explorers both past and present certainly talk in terms of an inward journey – the expedition as a voyage of self-discovery has become a polar platitude. A favourite aphorism

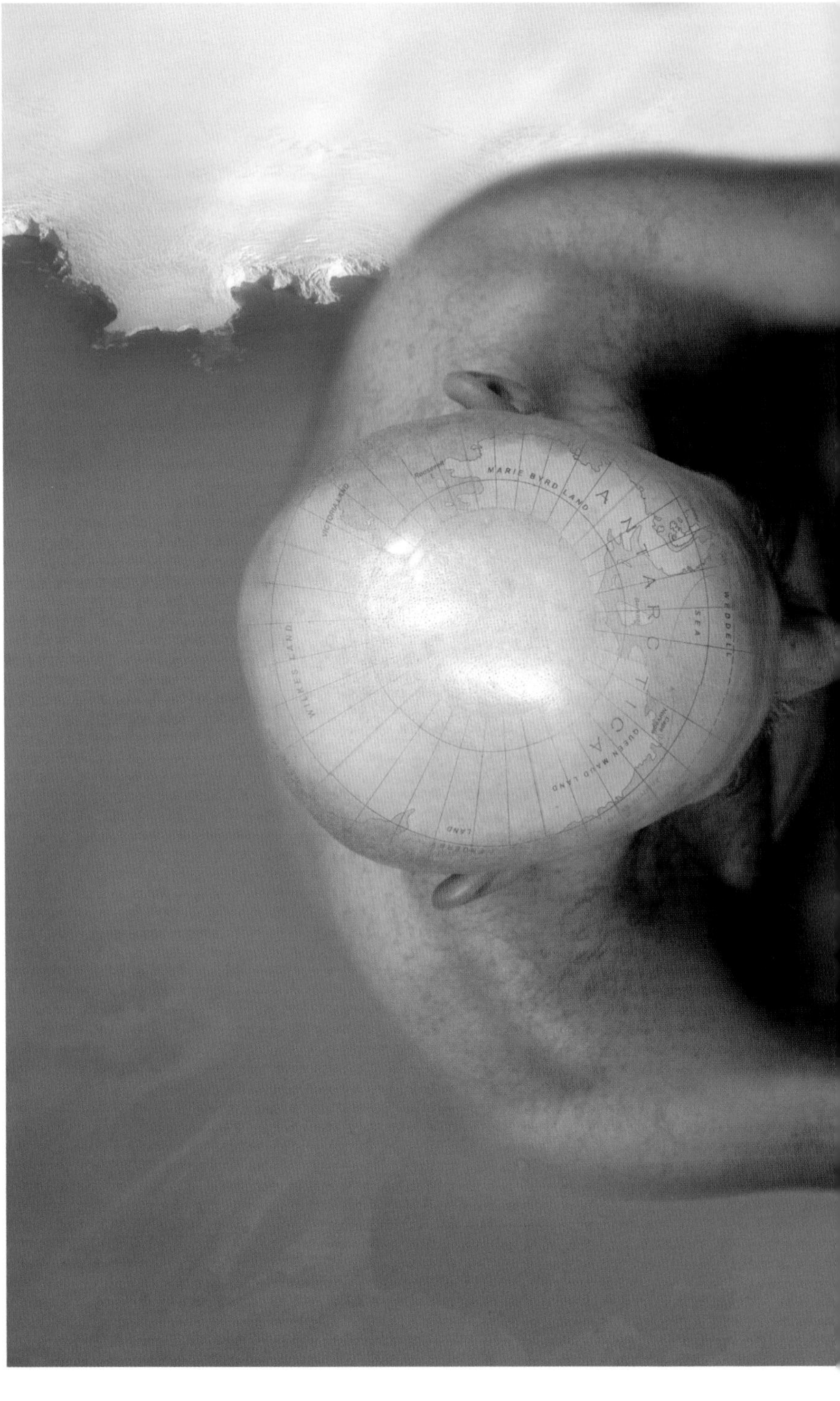
MARIE BYRD LAND
ANTARCTICA
WEDDELL
SEA
QUEEN MAUD LAND
WILKES LAND

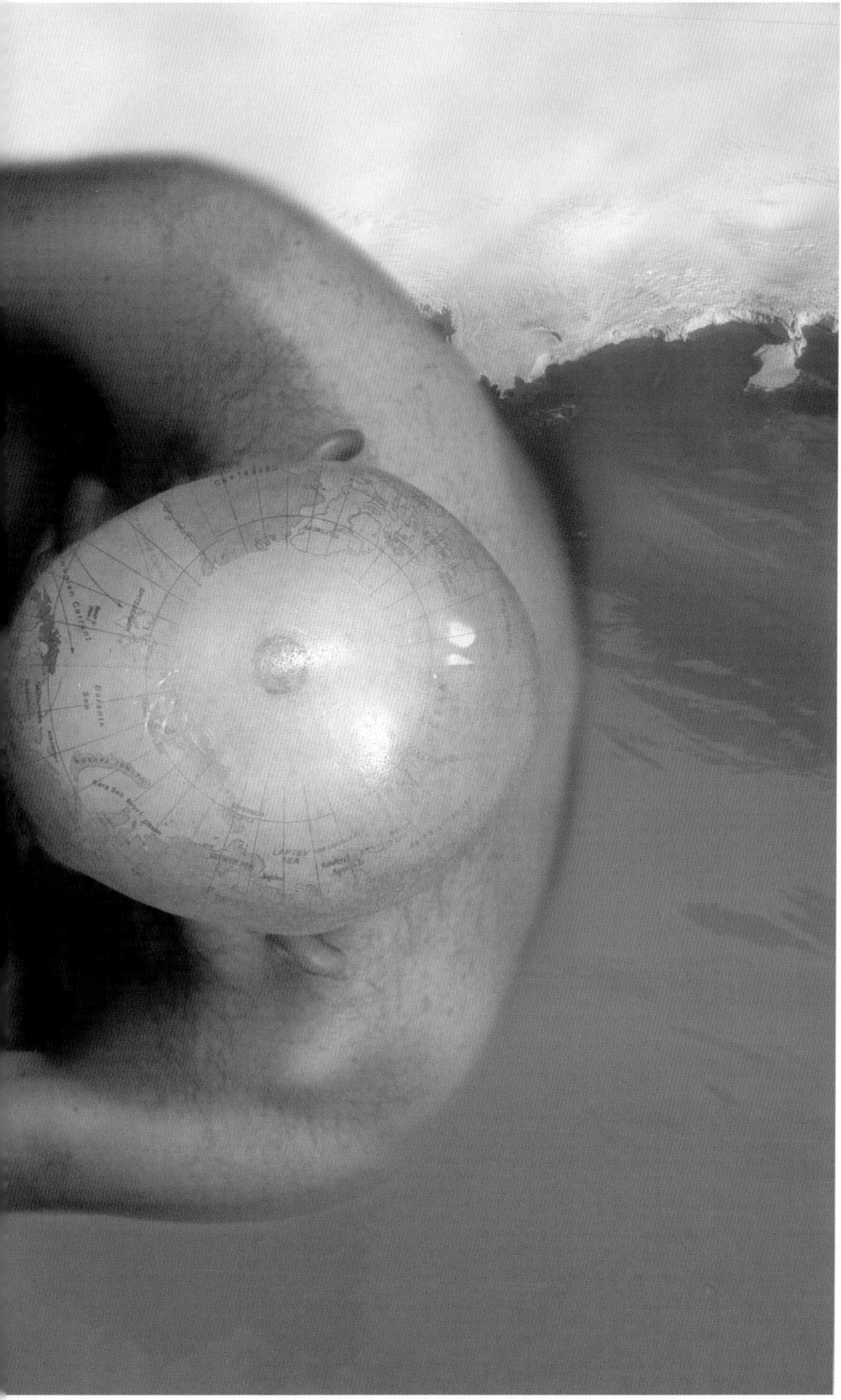
LAPTEV
SEA

repeated in memoirs and narratives is Ernest Shackleton's reflection: 'We all have our own White South.' The quotation itself may well be mythical, as its source, if it exists, is never supplied.[27] It is nonetheless echoed by many contemporary polar travellers. The British adventurer Ranulph Fiennes asserts: 'there is something of the South Pole in the hearts of all of us.'[28] The Norwegian Erling Kagge concurs: 'My travel across a part of Antarctica became more of a travel into myself, than to the pole itself . . . I believe everyone should find their own south poles.'[29] 'You wait. Everyone has an Antarctic', muses an old imperial explorer more ominously in Thomas Pynchon's novel *V* (1963). Seeking to 'stand at the dead centre of the carousel, if only for a moment; [to] try to catch my bearings', he finds at the Pole not the integration of the self but 'Nothing . . . a dream of annihilation'.[30]

In the title of his first expedition narrative, *The Heart of the Antarctic*, Shackleton identifies the Pole as the affective, if not the literal, centre of the continent. By his time it was well accepted that the Pole would harbour no open sea, no stupendous vortex, no magnetic mountain – just a featureless point on a plateau. Mythologies no longer focused on what marvellous thing might be located there, or what unimaginable insights it might offer, but rather on the meaning of having reached the point: the symbolic achievement of full geographic mastery. The Pole was the 'last frontier', the 'end of the Earth', the 'last place on Earth'. While this 'last' was technically disposed of by Roald Amundsen, it lingered in the sense of 'most remote', 'most isolated', 'most extreme'. Later in the century, with rising environmental consciousness, Antarctica became the 'last wilderness'. In post-apocalyptic films and novels, it is a 'last refuge' in a devastated world and/or a 'last hope' for a new one.

The mythology of the South Pole as the 'last place' is so pervasive that many would find it difficult to recognize it *as* a mythology rather than a literal fact. The cultural critic Elena Glasberg argues that the 'place-ideas' attached to the continent and the Pole 'had more to do with coincidence than any necessary properties of place'. There are parts of Earth less habitable,

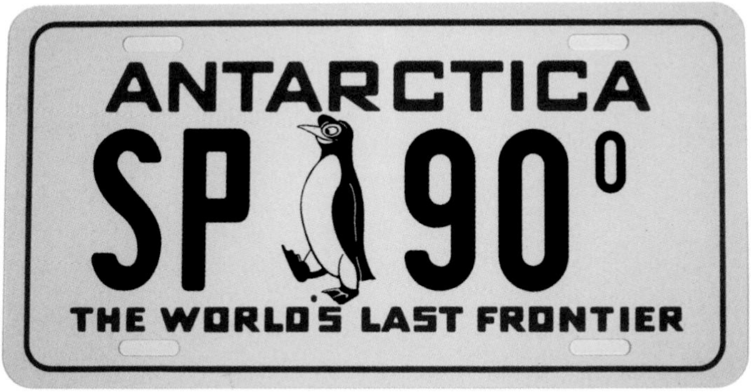

A novelty South Pole licence plate.

less explored, more difficult to get to – she points to certain mountainous regions and the ocean depths; deep cave systems are another example. Due to historical circumstance, however, 'the South Pole as the last place on earth has been invested with the aura of transcendence and promise of the completion of knowledge'. Since this completion is never possible, 'geographical attainments in fact only led to further attempts, arrivals, gestures of closure'.[31] One obvious example of the attainment of the 'end' merely producing a new stream of arrivals is the many polar traverses made in the 'footsteps' of famous explorers.

More than a century after Amundsen's team calculated that they had arrived in the vicinity of the Pole, new mapping and visualization technologies have inevitably altered perspectives of the continent and its symbolic centre. There is now a webcam at the South Pole and you can see images of various parts of the scientific station on Google Street View. When you turn to Google Earth, however, problems occur: the area around the Pole, including the station itself, is just a grey-white pixelated mess. Online conspiracy theorists inevitably link this anomaly to the hollow earth, aliens and the CIA. Geospatial experts point to the absence of high-resolution satellites that pass over the poles, as well as the process Google uses to map its imagery onto a virtual globe, which preferences accuracy at the equator, and produces a low resolution south of around 82 degrees. We are back, in a sense, where this chapter started, with maps that favour the middle of the Earth and push the South Polar region

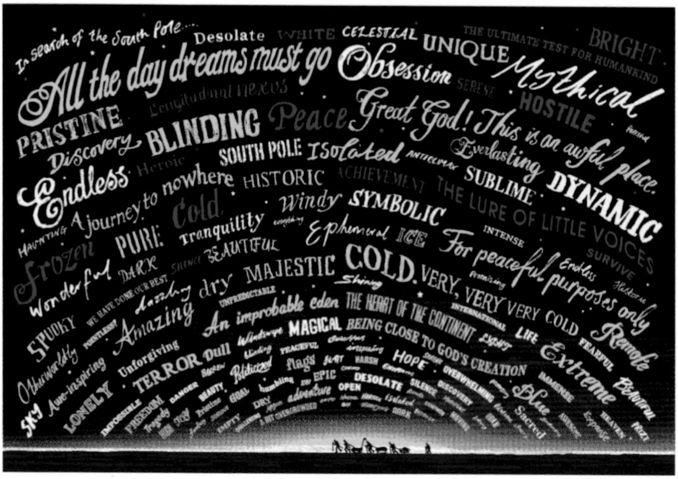

Andy Smith's image *Polar Sky*, created for the endpapers of the book *In Search of the South Pole* (2011), incorporates words used by explorers, scientists and travellers to describe the Pole.

off the bottom. In the digital age 90 degrees south continues to create problems for conventional cartographic representations.

Humanity's representation of the South Pole remains the same in another way, too: it is still on the 'bottom' of the Earth. Among the most famous photographs of our planet from space is *Earthrise*, one of several similar images taken by the *Apollo 8* astronauts in 1968. There was a problem, however, with the original colour photograph that offered the best image: the astronaut had taken it as he saw it, with the moon's surface in the vertical plane, meaning that its shadow over the Earth (positioned to its left) was also roughly vertical. To make the image a 'moonrise' it had to be rotated 90 degrees, so that the moon's surface was horizontal; but this put the Earth itself 'on its side'. In late 1972 another influential image taken from space, by the *Apollo 17* astronauts, entered into circulation. Where *Earthrise* shows an Earth half in the moon's shadow, this one showed the whole of one side of the sunlit planet, with Africa and the Arabian Peninsula in the upper part of the globe and Antarctica, under swirling clouds, clearly visible beneath. Moreover, it was taken with the Earth's axis in the vertical – although, with no other object in the frame, it could be rotated at will anyway. Known as *The Blue Marble*, this image became 'perhaps even more iconic' than *Earthrise*.[32] This was closer to the Earth that people recognized

The Blue Marble, original orientation.

from maps: 'no other photograph ever made of planet Earth has ever felt at-once so momentous and somehow so manageable, so *companionable*'.[33] The impact of this image on environmental understandings of Earth – as something holistic, isolated and vulnerable – is frequently remarked. Less often acknowledged is the fact that, in the version of *The Blue Marble* originally taken from the spacecraft, the South Pole is on top.

3 Polar Imaginations

> 'On this 21st day of March 1868, I, Captain Nemo, have reached the South Pole and the 90th degree, and I take possession of this part of the globe, now comprising one-sixth of all the discovered continents.'
> 'In whose name, captain?'
> 'In my own, monsieur!'[1]

It is both ironic and fitting that the first official claiming of the South Pole in literature should be made in the name of 'Nemo' – Latin for 'no one'. The mysterious and misanthropic submarine captain of Jules Verne's *Twenty Thousand Leagues Under the Seas* (1869–70), who normally avoids stepping on land, makes an exception of the small islet he discovers at the Geographic Pole, on the basis that it has not yet been sullied by a human foot. A political subversive, he refuses to claim this land for a nation, empire or sovereign, instead planting his own black flag with a golden 'N' as the sun sinks below the horizon at the autumnal equinox.

While Nemo may be the first fictional character to *claim* the South Pole, he was not the first to *reach* it. It is difficult to know to whom this particular credit should go. In Dante's *Inferno*, the first part of his fourteenth-century poem *The Divine Comedy*, the Greek literary hero Ulysses (now in the underworld) relates his final, fatal, voyage southwest towards 'the stars / of the other pole'.[2] He recalls having spied a mountain higher than any he had previously seen, before his ship, encountering a whirlwind, went down. Dante's whirlwind is a variation on the mythological South Polar vortex that besets many literary voyagers. The protagonist of an anonymous early eighteenth-century French novel, *Relation d'un voyage du Pole Arctique, au Pole Antarctique*, finds his vessel sucked down a tremendous whirlpool at the North Pole, rushed along 'terrifying torrents' in 'subterranean passages', whence it emerges in a calm, foggy sea at the other end of the Earth. In the Antarctic regions the sailors encounter flying fish as large as cows and architectural evidence of intelligent life.[3]

What this French fantastic voyage only gestures towards, other early narratives are keen to describe in detail: a native South Polar people. They make their first appearance in what is often cited as the earliest 'Antarctic' work of fiction, Bishop Joseph Hall's *Mundus alter et idem* (1605), a dystopian satire set in a southern continent that sprawls from the equator to the Pole. The people inhabiting the far southern region of Moronia are, as the name suggests, rather stupid. Unsurprisingly, given that they live in a cold, icy land shrouded in 'nearly perpetual' darkness, they prefer to stay indoors, dwelling on what they might have done or could have been.[4] Other inhabitants of the region are more exotic and more sinister: 'frenzied' cannibalistic savages, witches, werewolves and ghosts.[5]

Captain Nemo plants his flag at the South Pole in Alphonse de Neuville's illustration to Jules Verne's *Twenty Thousand Leagues Under the Seas* (1870).

Growing evidence from exploratory expeditions that the far south was hostile to life made comparatively little impact on fiction over the following centuries. Novelists refused to give up such a productive idea as an inhabited Antarctic, often positing instead an icy barrier enclosing a temperate or even tropical land, or an open sea dotted with islands. Even a novelist as careful of factual detail as Verne has a group of marooned sailors drifting over the Pole on an iceberg in *Les sphinx des glaces* (1897). Speculations about a liveable polar environment were given a credibility of sorts by developing scientific and geographic knowledge. The possibility of geothermal heat was raised in 1841 when James Clark Ross's expedition happened on one of the regions' few active volcanoes, the smoking Ere-

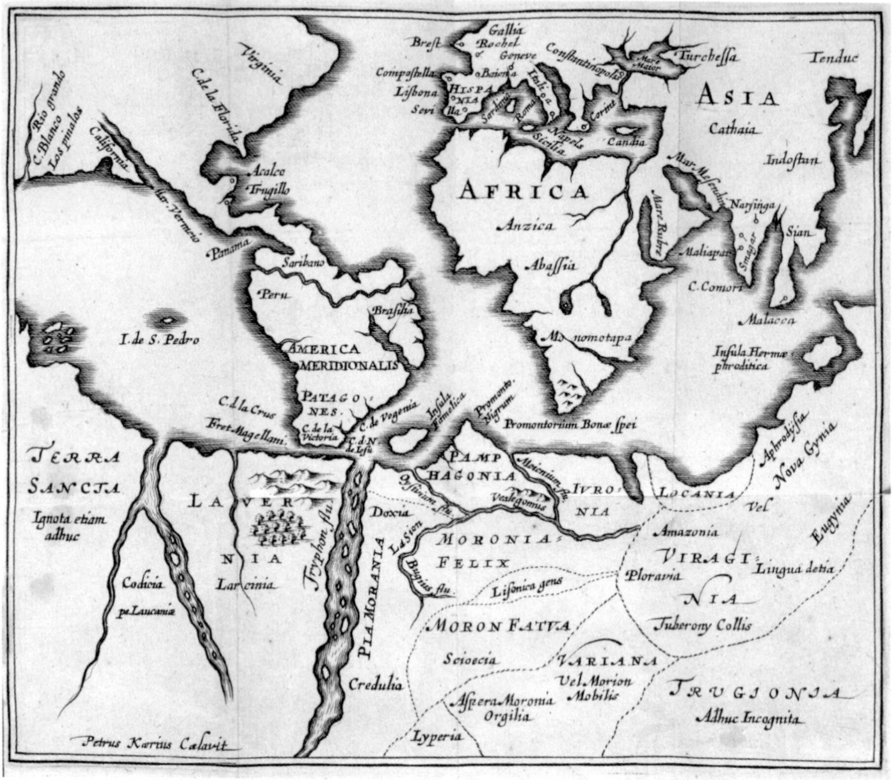

World map from Joseph Hall's *Mundus alter et idem* (1643 edition).

bus. Understanding of the Earth's 'squashed sphere' shape – which means that the poles are comparatively close to the planet's core – similarly bolstered the suggestion that the high latitudes offered unusual access to underground heat sources, fuelling fantasies of an ice-free, temperate (or even tropical) polar environment. 'Lost race' stories dominated Antarctic fiction in the late 1800s and continued well into the twentieth century.

The South Polar region has thus been home to all manner of fictional beings: hermaphrodites in Gabriel de Foigny's *Australe connue* (The Southern Land, Known, 1676); flying people in Roger Paltock's *The Life and Adventures of Peter Wilkins* (1750); intelligent monkeys in James Fenimore Cooper's *The Monikins* (1835); a treacherous jet-black tribe in Edgar Allan Poe's *The Narrative of Arthur Gordon Pym of Nantucket* (1838); descendants of ancient Greeks, ancient Romans and sixteenth-century Englishmen in various late nineteenth-century texts (Eugene Bisbee's *The Treasure of the Ice*, 1888; Charles Romyn Dake's *Strange Discovery*, 1899; Edward Bouvé's *Centuries Apart*, 1894); 'Antarctic Esquimaux' who speak Maori in Julius Vogel's *Anno Dominis 2000* (1899); dinosaurs in Frank Savile's *Beyond the Great South Wall* (1901) and John Taine's *The Greatest Adventure* (1929); giant insects, giant intelligent crabs and giant humanoid lobsters in pulp science-fiction magazine stories of the 1930s; Neanderthals and Cro-Magnon men in Edison Marshall's *Dian of the Lost Land* (1935); leprechauns and Satanists in Dennis Wheatley's *The Man Who Missed the War* (1945); ageing Nazis in M. E. Morris's *The Icemen* (1988); and giant radioactive elephant seals in Matthew Reilly's *Ice Station* (1998).

Just as attractive as the idea of indigenous people near the South Pole was the possibility of lucrative commercial prospects. While the resources of the far southern ocean and the Antarctic islands – whales and seals – were vigorously exploited, producing literary responses such as James Fenimore Cooper's *The Sea Lions* (1849), nobody knew what the region around the Pole itself might offer. The narrator of Daniel Defoe's fictional travel tale *A New Voyage round the World* (1724), sailing in subantarctic waters, relates the rumour that 'if there was any Land directly under the Poles, either *South* or *North*, there wou'd be found Gold of a Fineness more than Double to any that was ever yet found in the World'. He remains sceptical, however, partly due to lack of evidence, and partly because no one could ever reach the spot, which is surrounded by 'Mountains of Snow, and frozen Seas which never Thaw'.[6] Nevertheless the allure remained. In Christopher Spotswood's late nineteenth-century utopia, *Voyage of Will Rogers to the South Pole* (1888), the temperate polar land of Bencolo harbours plentiful precious metals, and Rogers happily pockets the five pounds of gold presented to him by his Antarctic friends.[7] The protagonist of George McIver's *Neuroomia* (1894) easily digs up a large nugget of Antarctic gold, predicting that 'if it were known in the other continents that gold was so plentiful in Neuroomia, there would be a rush of a few millions of people to these parts, if only to perish on the ice.'[8] By the mid-twentieth century the focus had changed only slightly: 'Several Governments have an eye on the South Pole', observes the flying detective hero of W. E. Johns's *Biggles Breaks the Silence* (1949), 'and that's nothing to wonder at . . . nobody knows what metals, coal and oil there may be in that ground for the first nation to tame it'.[9]

" Where's that gold ? " See page 150.

One of Leslie Stead's illustrations to W. E. Johns's *Biggles Breaks the Silence.*

Biggles is here equating the South Pole with the continent of Antarctica, not 90 degrees south. While the Geographic Pole itself may have national, political, geographic, scientific and psychological significance, it has little obvious commercial value. There are no seals or whales to be found, and any minerals are under miles of ice and far harder to retrieve than in other parts of the continent. When the title character of Victor Appleton II's *Tom Swift and his Atomic Earth Blaster* (1954) decides to go to the 'South Pole' to mine iron, he too is using the term loosely; he fires up his 'blaster' somewhere near the Transantarctic Mountains. Although Antarctic fiction shifted in the later twentieth century from adventure novels and lost-race romances to eco-, techno- and political thrillers, these novels too are normally set in relatively accessible parts of the continent, rather than at the Pole.

For many creative writers the Antarctic was simply a generic blank space in which to set their narratives and the South Pole its most exotic point. Fictional heroes of serial adventures – Tarzan, the Hardy Boys, Doctor Who – inevitably visit at some stage, adding it to one of their many far-flung destinations. Other writers, however, were more interested in the specifics of the place, drawing on the long-standing symbolic associations of the Pole. Unlike the Arctic, which, in the Western geographic imagination, sits 'on top' of the Earth, the Antarctic hangs underneath, with the South Pole at its nadir, inevitably evoking a sense of being 'upside-down'. This is what attracted early utopianists and satirists to the Great Southern Land – it was an ideal place in which to depict a society that metaphorically turned one's own on its head. Nicolas-Edmé Rétif de la Bretonne's *La découverte australe par un homme-volant* (Austral Discovery by a Flying Man, 1781) features the high-latitude land of 'Megapatagonia' where 'all is upside-down and back-to-front'.[10] Cooper's intelligent monkeys – or 'monikins' – have their brains in their tails. *A Strange Manuscript Found in a Copper Cylinder* (1888), by Canadian novelist James De Mille, features an Antarctica occupied by a contrarian people who worship darkness and practise pathological self-denial. The idea is taken to its logical extreme in a short story by Russian writer Valery Bryusov entitled (in English translation) 'The Republic of the Southern Cross' (1905). The citizens of the Republic's capital, Zvezdny, located on the Pole itself, are struck by the disease of 'contradiction', which makes them act in precisely the opposite way to their intentions: people turn left rather than right; policemen confuse rather than direct traffic; doctors prescribe poison rather than medicine. As the disease reaches epidemic proportions, the city quickly descends into anarchy.

The front cover of *Tom Swift and his Atomic Earth Blaster* (1954).

Typical of this kind of up-ending are Antarctic narratives which reverse expected gender hierarchies. Adam More, the aptly named narrator of De Mille's anti-utopian satire, can cope with many of the perverse habits of the native Antarctic Kosekin – 'Their love of darkness, their passion for death, their contempt of riches, their yearning after unrequited love, their human sacrifices, their cannibalism' – but draws the line at females taking the initiative: 'that a woman should propose to a man

– it really was more than a fellow could stand'.[11] The hero of Frank Cowan's *Revi-Lona* (privately published in the 1880s) takes a different approach when he discovers 'a perfect but petticoated paradise' at the South Pole. Revelling in being a 'big and brawny' newcomer in a society where men are 'little and learned' and women large, beautiful and dominant, he fathers 98 children from 40 women in his six-year stay.[12] He connects the female-dominated society with the topsy-turvy nature of their land: 'you embody the surroundings of the southern pole of the planet, I embody the environment of the northern hemisphere.'[13]

If, for some novelists, the South Pole signalled an upside-down world, for others it suggested an inside-out one. John Cleves Symmes Jr's claim that the Earth was hollow, with a habitable interior accessed via large, ice-rimmed holes at the poles, was too suggestive of imaginative possibilities for novelists to ignore. The first fictionalization of the theory appeared just a couple of years after Symmes had circulated his initial pamphlet: *Symzonia* (1820) opens with the narrator and supposed author, Adam Seaborn, bemoaning the lack of blank spaces remaining on the Earth's surface. Equipping himself with Symmes's writings, he heads south. Having passed through the southern polar hole, his expedition discovers a utopian (and startlingly white-skinned) people blessed with bountiful resources. The author behind the obvious pseudonym has never been determined, with some critics arguing that the novel was written by Symmes himself to promote his theory, and others that it satirizes his ideas.

The polar hole down which Seaborn's ship sails smoothly, the crew barely noticing the transition from outer to inner realm, seems a far cry from the legendary whirlpools that medieval sailors feared. But when Edgar Allan Poe, writing in the interval between Symmes's proposal and the first official U.S. exploring expedition to the far southern regions, took up the idea, the polar vortex returned in all of its sublime terror. The narrator of his 'MS Found in a Bottle' (1833) finds himself (through a series of maritime accidents) on a seemingly supernatural ship sucked by a 'strong current, or impetuous undertow' towards the South

Pole: 'we are hurrying onwards to some exciting knowledge – some never-to-be-imparted secret, whose attainment is destruction'.[14] The story ends abruptly with the narrator plummeting down a gigantic whirlpool (presumably maintaining the presence of mind to stuff his account into a bottle at the last moment). The protagonist of Poe's only novel, *The Narrative of Arthur Gordon Pym of Nantucket* (1838), ends his eventful and traumatic South Polar voyage in a similarly dramatic fashion: with his boat rushing towards a 'limitless cataract', he is confronted by a mysterious, giant, perfectly white human figure.[15] For Poe the South Pole is a place of simultaneous annihilation and vision, catastrophic destruction and ultimate insight.

The notion of a polar vortex in one sense obliterates the Pole itself: no longer a place on the Earth's surface, it becomes the midpoint of a gaping hole, the centre of nothingness. Yet at the same time this idea gives the Pole an identity: instead of a point on a featureless snowscape, unidentifiable except through complex calculations, it is marked by a striking natural feature. Moreover, the vortex transforms the Pole from an end to a means: rather than the final point of a journey, it becomes the key to a new space – a gateway to another, interior world. Portals of various kinds recur in Antarctic fiction, with writers often bestowing ingenious or ludicrous topologies upon the world's southernmost point. In *The Monikins* the Pole acts as a kind of valve that lets off steam from the Earth's interior.[16] Thomas Erskine's utopian satire *Armata* (1817) is set on a sister planet connected to Earth by a watery channel at (it appears) the South Pole, so that the two globes are joined like 'a double-headed shot'.[17] Later writers scale this idea up to an interplanetary level. In Gustavus Pope's *Journey to Mars* (1894), stranded explorers are rescued by Martian visitors who exploit the 'Cosmo-magnetic currents' between the poles of Earth and its neighbour for their travels.

As these examples make clear, before Amundsen and his team reached the South Pole in late 1911, all literary representations of this place were inescapably speculative. Realistic depictions of the Antarctic continent necessarily stopped at its coastline. Samuel Taylor Coleridge, who grounded his gothic horror ballad 'The

'Attacked by bears'. Illustration from W.H.G Kingston's *At the South Pole*.

Rime of the Ancient Mariner' (1798) in detail gathered from travel narratives of the far north as well as the south, goes no further than the sea ice. Cooper set his utopian satire *The Monikins* on fictional lands near the Pole, but the main action of his second, more realistic Antarctic novel *The Sea Lions* – a nautical adventure narrative and morality tale about the rival captains of two sealing expeditions – takes place on an unspecified island near the polar circle.

However, novelists who eschewed the fantastic conceits of flying people, lost tribes, polar vortexes and routes to Mars were left to contend with the problem of creating drama in an environment emptied of many of its traditional sources. The boys' adventure novelist W.H.G. Kingston did his best in *At the South Pole* (1870), putting his troubled whaling crew through a fearsomely cold Antarctic winter, an encounter with a wrecked Portuguese vessel from a long-gone era, volcanic eruptions and close calls with colliding and overturning icebergs, but to sustain his narrative he also added wolves, outsized walruses and enormous polar bears, transposing far northern threats to the largely unknown south. When exotic (and exoticized) elements are not

Front cover of Gordon Stables's *In the Great White Land* (first edition, 1903).

IN THE GREAT
WHITE LAND

simply found in the fictional Antarctic, they can be transported there as part of the narrative: the American hero of Gordon Stables's *In the Great White Land* (1903) equips his expedition with a group of hardy indigenous Arctic nomads called 'Yak-yaks' along with their 'Yak-dogs'; four young polar bears trained to pull a sled; two St Bernards; a Scotch collie; and several Shetland ponies. His trek to the South Pole (enabled by a trusty Yak-yak) is forestalled by the discovery of a frozen sea stretching over the region.

In the same year that British boys thrilled to the adventures reported in Stables's novel, the naval officer Robert F. Scott led the first serious attempt to reach the South Pole. In the following two decades, a slew of expeditions (mostly European) tried to cross the ice without mechanical aids, using man- or dog-power to cover vast amounts of territory in an attempt to know and claim the southern continent. This period has come to be termed, almost always with qualifying quotation marks, the 'Heroic Era' of Antarctic exploration. It drew adventure novelists up short as the reality of South Polar exploration produced non-fictional narratives that rivalled, in their ability to hold the public imagination, anything produced by creative writers.

4 Pole-hunting

In one early twentieth-century novel, an Antarctic explorer named Anthony Dyke outlines his sole burning ambition to his besotted mistress:

> He went on, in his vibrating heart-stirring whisper, to speak of the South Pole . . . Dyke meant, had always meant, to capture the South Pole, and all other tasks were but a filling or wasting of time. He had marked it down as his own. He spoke of it as if it had been some dangerous yet timid animal of the chase, round which he had made narrowing circles till it crouched, fascinated, unable any more to flee from its pursuer; it knew that it could not escape and that when Dyke ceased to circle and dashed in, it must fall into his hands.[1]

This metaphor – the explorer as a safari hunter, the South Pole as his quarry – is from one perspective absurd: in what way is an invisible, stationary point like a dangerous crouching animal? In another sense, however, it is quite apt, evoking the culture of imperial adventure and masculine endeavour in which early journeys into the continent were inevitably embedded. Reaching the South Pole was not only a quest, it was a conquest, even if its defeated subject was an abstract spot on an entirely lifeless plateau. Roald Amundsen (whose voyage narratives were the factual sources for Dyke's fictional adventures[2]) draws on the language of chivalry rather than safari when describing the quest for the South Pole, but constructs a similarly violent image. The main aim of early Antarctic explorers, he writes, was 'to strike the Antarctic monster – in the heart, if fortune favoured them'.[3] It was, of course, Amundsen himself who struck the final blow.

Like most exploration narratives, Amundsen's *The South Pole* (1912) provides a potted history of previous attempts to explore the Antarctic region – a South Polar genealogy. He divides it into two stages. The first comprises voyagers who headed south with only vague notions of what the region might yield: this group includes Bartolomeu Dias, Vasco da Gama, Ferdinand Magellan, Francis Drake, Edmond Halley and Jean-Baptiste-Charles Bouvet de Lozier. The next group, 'Antarctic travellers in the proper sense of the term', were more purposeful – these were the men aiming at the monster's heart.[4] This second stage ends, implicitly, with Amundsen's own triumphant journey, the subject of his book; but it begins with British naval captain James Cook.

On his second world voyage, in the *Resolution* and *Adventure* (1772–5), Cook was charged with investigating land sighted at 54 degrees south in 1739 by Bouvet de Lozier. The Frenchman believed a 'cape' he had discovered could be a part of a southern continent. If this proved to be the case, Cook was to investigate and to befriend any natives; if not, he should continue southwards, still looking for the continent, 'keeping in as high a latitude as

Bronze bust of Amundsen outside the Institute for Marine and Antarctic Studies, Hobart. The original plaster work was made by the American sculptor Victor Lewis in 1921. This cast was brought to Tasmania by the Norwegian navigator Einar Sverre Pedersen in 1988.

First edition of Amundsen's expedition narrative (1912).

I could, and prosecuting my discoveries as near to the South Pole as possible'. Unable to find Bouvet de Lozier's cape and believing it to have been simply a large iceberg (it was later discovered to be a tiny, isolated island), Cook continued southwards, making the first ever crossing of the polar circle in early 1773. Over the following two years he circumnavigated the continent for the first time, dipping down to more than 71 degrees south in early 1774. At this point he was confronted by numerous 'ice-hills . . . looking like a ridge of mountains, rising one above another till they were lost in the clouds'. He abandoned the attempt to approach the Pole, and not without some relief:

> there must be some [land] to the South behind this ice; but if there is, it can afford no better retreat for birds, or any other animals, than the ice itself, with which it must be wholly covered. I, who had ambition not only to go farther

> than any one had been before, but as far as it was possible for man to go, was not sorry at meeting with this interruption.[5]

During the following decades it was sailors hunting for seals who most often ventured into high southern latitudes, quickly exhausting the populations of various subantarctic islands and pushing further south. Operating in a competitive industry, these sealers were not keen to advertise their discoveries, with the result that the first sighting of and landing on the continent are hard to pinpoint; there are several contenders for both. The earliest sighting is often attributed to Thaddeus von Bellingshausen, an explorer in the Russian navy, in late January 1820, but this is highly contestable. An American sealing expedition led by John Davis is usually considered to have made the first continental landing in February 1821. Another sealer, James Weddell, passed Cook's 'farthest south' in 1823, reaching over 74 degrees south in surprisingly fine, ice-free conditions, turning back not due to obstacles but rather the 'lateness of the season' and the knowledge of a perilous homeward journey. It was, he speculated, 'at least probable' that the Pole was covered by water, and hence could be reached by sea.[6] These and other achievements by sealers obviously added to knowledge of the Antarctic, but this group of voyagers were not focused on the Pole itself – or only inasmuch as it might (if Weddell's experience was indicative) harbour more unsuspecting seals.

Frontispiece to the narrative of Dumont d'Urville's expedition (1837–40).

Pole-hunting, not seal-hunting, was a crucial impetus for three naval exploratory expeditions sent south by France, the U.S. and Britain respectively in the late 1830s. Jules Dumont d'Urville, who led the French expedition, was instructed to 'extend [his] exploration towards the Pole as far as the polar ice will permit'.[7] His crewmen were offered

Sketched by Dr. Hooker.
Catching the Great Penguins. Page 159.

Illustration from Ross's *A Voyage of Discovery* (1847). Several emperor penguins were caught and brought on board ship, where they were killed and (in some instances) preserved in cases of pickle for further study.

100 francs each if the expedition reached 75 degrees south, with a bonus of 5 francs for each further degree south.[8] The American expedition, under Charles Wilkes, was instructed to follow 'the track of Weddell as closely as practicable . . . endeavouring to reach a high southern latitude'.[9] While neither expedition came close to Weddell's record, they charted significant areas of the Antarctic coast elsewhere; both also gave (inaccurate) estimates of the position of the Magnetic South Pole. The instructions given to James Clark Ross, leader of the British expedition to the Antarctic, were more tightly focused on the Magnetic Pole – the position of which the German mathematician Carl Friedrich Gauss had recently predicted. After establishing magnetic observatories and taking measurements in various locations, he was to 'proceed direct to the southward' in order to determine its position, 'and even to attain it, if possible'.[10]

It was not possible, by ship at least: unbeknown to Ross until he reached the Antarctic region, the Magnetic Pole at this time lay inland, and his ships could not get closer to it than around 300 km (160 nautical miles).[11] However, Ross's men did not come away disappointed: they bettered Weddell's farthest south (at a different longitude); discovered what is now known as the Ross Sea; encountered and claimed new coastline (Victoria Land); sailed along the spectacular ice cliffs of the 'Victoria Barrier' (now the Ross Ice Shelf); and sighted two volcanic peaks, which they named Erebus and Terror after their ships. The area of land on which these volcanoes sat (now known as Ross Island) became the launching point for later British attempts on the Geographic Pole, and the Ross Ice Shelf was to be Amundsen's base for his successful polar journey.

For around the next half-century, there was little interest in reaching either the Magnetic or the Geographic South Pole, although scientific investigation in the Antarctic region was maintained by the *Challenger* oceanographic expedition. Subantarctic sealing continued on a significantly reduced scale (the original populations had been decimated) and whalers did not often venture into the far south until the later nineteenth century. Whaling and sealing were intended to underwrite the expense of the next expedition to reach Antarctica, led by the Norwegian businessman Henryk Johan Bull. While the commercial results were disappointing, the explorers did at least step onto the continent, in 1894 at Cape Adare in Victoria Land, an event often cited as the first 'official' landing. Bull concluded that it would be possible to spend a 'safe and pleasant' year at Cape Adare, with the possibility of reaching the Magnetic Pole.[12]

With the Sixth International Geographical Congress, in 1895, refocusing attention on Antarctica, numerous expeditions headed southwards over the next decade, although not all of them were safe or pleasant. Carsten Borchgrevink, a Norwegian-born Australian immigrant and one of the landing party on Bull's expedition, remained entranced by the 'glittering gates of the Poles'.[13] He took up his erstwhile leader's suggestion, spending the winter of 1899 at Cape Adare in charge of the British Antarctic Expedition. Only three of the ten wintering men were actually British; the expedition's national identification came from its sponsor, a British publishing magnate, who had contributed £40,000 to its funds.[14] Heroic feats in the polar regions made good press. Borchgrevink claimed, rather dubiously, to have fixed the location of the Magnetic South Pole, which had inevitably shifted since Ross's visit, and he made a short trek (about 10 miles) inland over the Barrier, achieving a new farthest south of 78°50´ (78 degrees 50 minutes south).[15] His expedition was the first to winter on the continent itself, although not the first in the Antarctic – the men of the *Belgica* expedition had spent a notoriously trying winter the previous year in their ice-entrapped ship.

Between 1900 and 1905 Scottish, French, German, Swedish and British expeditions arrived in the Antarctic, with several of these nations planning to coordinate efforts to take magnetic measurements in different regions. All had scientific and geographic goals, but only the British were located in an area that could enable a serious attempt on the Geographic South Pole. William Speirs Bruce, leader of the Scottish expedition, was in his own words 'not a pole hunter' nor someone who believed in 'urging men on till they drop in order to get a mile further north or south than somebody else'. His expedition undertook hydrographic research in the Weddell Sea.[16]

Robert F. Scott, who led the British National Antarctic Expedition (or *Discovery* expedition) of 1901–4, was no Pole-hunter either, at least initially. He was, in a sense, an accidental explorer. In his account of his first expedition, he confesses that prior to this journey he 'had no predilection for Polar exploration' and that the story of his selection as leader (as a young midshipman he had impressed the influential geographer Clements Markham) was 'exceedingly tame'.[17] With tension mounting between the geographic and scientific supporters of the expedition, the idea of attaining the Geographic South Pole itself was 'carefully avoided' in the expedition instructions,[18] and exploration of the region to the south of their base (on Ross Island) was listed as only one of a number of tasks. It was, however, implicitly an exciting potential outcome, if an aspirational one. Scott chose to lead the push southwards himself, accompanied by the expedition physician and zoologist Edward Wilson and third officer Ernest Shackleton, whose 'one ambition' was reportedly to 'go on the southern journey'. The three of them were, Wilson recorded privately, 'quite determined to do a big distance towards the South Pole'.[19]

They did cover a great distance – nearly 1,600 km (1,000 miles) for the round trip – but this included doubling over their tracks when they had to relay heavy loads. In late December

1902 they reached a record southern latitude of just over 82 degrees before turning back, but their journey was plagued with problems, including difficulty with their sledge dogs, whose food had spoiled. Eventually, they had to start killing some dogs to feed others – a process that Scott found appalling enough to make him wary of this method in future. The explorers themselves began to suffer from scurvy, and eventually Shackleton could only walk alongside the sledge or sit on it, pulled by the other two men. They had 'made a greater advance towards a pole of the earth than has ever yet been achieved by a sledge party', but they had not come within 800 km (500 miles) of the South Pole.[20]

While the expedition remained another winter, its ship (where the men lived) frozen into the ice, Shackleton was invalided home on a relief ship. The traumas of the southern journey, however, had evidently not turned him off polar exploration: by 1907 he had raised funds for his own expedition, and headed southwards that year in an old sealing vessel, the *Nimrod*. Basing himself at

'Antarctica; or, The Race to the South Pole' – National Game Company, *c.* 1905.

The makeshift flag used by David, Mawson and Mackay to mark their arrival at – or, at least, near – the Magnetic South Pole.

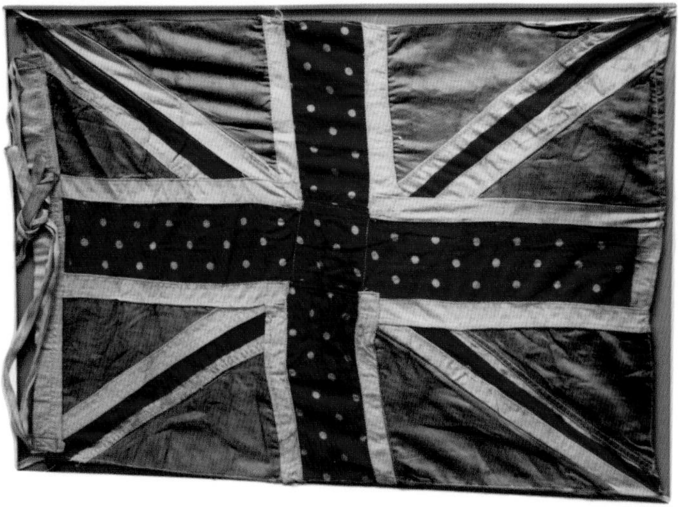

Cape Royds (also on Ross Island), Shackleton made a two-pronged attack on the poles: a three-man party led by the 50-year-old Australian geologist Edgeworth David headed over the mountains towards the Magnetic, while Shackleton with three others focused on the Geographic. Only the former reached their goal – more or less.

The journey to the Magnetic Pole was beset with difficulties. David's leadership style grated with the two younger men of the team, Douglas Mawson (whom David had taught at university) and Alistair Mackay, and his lesser strength and fitness were a problem. They had several dangerous encounters with crevasses, and their rations were insufficient for the journey, making them all obsessed with food. In early 1909, however, more than three months after their departure from base, they were nearing their frustratingly shifting goalpost. 'The compass . . . indicates that the polar centre executes a daily round of wanderings about its mean position', David wrote in a later account:

> Mawson considered that we were now practically at the Magnetic Pole, and that if we were to wait for twenty-four hours . . . the Pole would probably, during that time, come vertically beneath us. We decided, however, to go on to the

Jameson Adams, Frank Wild and Shackleton pose beside the Union Jack at their 'farthest south'. The fourth team member, Eric Marshall, took the photograph.

> spot where he concluded the approximate mean position of the Magnetic Pole would lie.[21]

As per Shackleton's instructions, they proclaimed the area part of the British Empire and raised a makeshift flag. There had been no spare Union Jack available for their voyage, so one had been 'very ingeniously' constructed prior to their departure from a red polka-dotted handkerchief and some curtain material.[22] They took a photograph of the moment using a string-pull, and, 'too utterly weary to be capable of any great amount of exultation', headed back.[23] The return leg had its share of difficulties, too: with David now 'partially demented', according to Mawson, Mackay urged the younger Australian to wrest leadership from his former teacher, to no avail.[24] They arrived at base around four months after they had left, having covered 2,030 km (1,260 miles). Two years later, it was shown that they had come close to, but not within, the Magnetic Pole's area of oscillation.[25] However, posterity has tended to consider it near enough.

While David's team was trekking towards one pole, Shackleton's was aiming at another. Using Manchurian ponies rather than dogs to haul supplies, Shackleton led his team across the Barrier and up the Beardmore Glacier onto the plateau. As the journey continued, the men suffering from hunger and the hostile conditions, it became clear that they could not reach the Pole and return alive. About a week before David, Mawson and Mackay reached the Magnetic Pole, Shackleton decided to turn away from the Geographic one, but not before making a last desperate dash southwards to make sure the team reached a point within 185 km (100 nautical miles) of their goal. Marching further would have meant certain death and, as he later joked to his wife, he felt she would prefer 'a live donkey' to 'a dead lion'.[26]

It was not the announcement of Shackleton's failure to reach the South Pole in March 1909 but reports the following September of Frederick Cook's and then Robert Peary's claims to have reached the North Pole that sent Amundsen south. Amundsen *was* a Pole-hunter; but it was the top, not the bottom, of the world that initially lured him: 'The regions around the North Pole – well, yes, the North Pole itself – had attracted me from childhood'. On hearing that he could not (as it then appeared) be first to the North Pole, he quickly decided 'to turn to the right-about, and face to the South'.[27] The Norwegian explorer had been in the Antarctic before, on the *Belgica* expedition. He also had extensive Arctic experience, having led the first expedition to negotiate the Northwest Passage early in the twentieth century, during which he spent instructive time with Inuit people. He was planning to reach the North Pole by drifting in a ship in the polar ice and had convinced the prominent explorer Fridtjof Nansen to provide his ship *Fram* for the purpose, when he received the startling news of its prior discovery.

Amundsen, *c.* 1913.

In a move that would create considerable controversy, Amundsen did not announce his abrupt change of direction, even to Nansen. According to his own account, in order to prevent media debate he initially told his plans only to his brother and the *Fram*'s captain.[28] Most of the crew members believed they would, as per the original plans, journey southwards through the Atlantic, east round Cape Horn and thence northwards to the Arctic, starting from this location in order to exploit the ice pack's drift. But rather than east, the ship turned west around the Cape of Good Hope, having stopped at Madeira, where the startled but willing crew was informed of the new aim, and letters were written back to Norway announcing the change. Amundsen's brother Leon, who had met the ship in Madeira, was instructed

This cartoon by Frank Nankivell from *Puck* magazine (1909) shows the North Pole leaving the 'Ranks of the Undiscovered'. The South Pole remains behind, along with 'Universal Peace' and 'The Great American Novel'.

to send (upon his return to Norway) a now-famous telegram to Scott: 'Beg leave to inform you *Fram* proceeding Antarctic. Amundsen.'

The *Fram* proceeded to the Bay of Whales, arriving in early 1910. Amundsen had decided to establish his base 'Framheim' not on land but on the floating Ross Ice Shelf, about 60 miles (96 km) closer to the Pole than Ross Island. He planned an early start for his southern journey the following spring: 'If we had set out to capture this record, we must at any cost get there first. Everything must be staked on this.'[29] Their first attempt in September 1911, however, was too early – the extreme cold drove the eight-man party back to base. They tried again in mid-October, with five men: Amundsen, Helmer Hanssen, Sverre Hassel, Oscar Wisting and Olav Bjaaland. On this second attempt, progress was much better. With all the men using skis, and dogs pulling supplies, their journey to the Pole, although it inevitably included encounters with crevasses and minor mishaps, was comparatively devoid of incident and danger.

On the afternoon of 14 December, just under two months after they left Framheim, Amundsen's drivers called a stop: 'They had carefully examined their sledge-meters, and they all showed the full distance – our Pole by reckoning. The goal was reached, the journey ended.' Not quite: as described in Chapter One, Amundsen took every effort to come as close to 90 degrees south as possible. Having raised a Norwegian flag, claimed the area in the name of King Haakon VII and set up tent, he took observations and sent out skiers to ensure that one of them came near the exact spot. Eventually, on 17 December, they settled on a location, which they named 'Polheim'. Here they set up their spare tent, finding inside it hidden messages of congratulations sewn in by their confident expedition-mates: 'Welcome to 90°'.[30] They enjoyed cigars, took photographs and left in the tent a letter to King Haakon along with a note to Scott asking him to relay it, in case they met with accident on their return leg.

While Amundsen's team was returning to base in the early part of January 1912, the *Fram*, waiting for them at the Bay of Whales, unexpectedly encountered another exploratory vessel:

Members of the Japanese expedition to Antarctica on board the *Kainan-maru*, 1910–12.

the *Kainan-maru*, carrying the Japanese South Polar Expedition, led by army lieutenant Nobu Shirase. Shirase was another Pole-hunter. Like Amundsen, his focus had been on the north until Cook and Peary forestalled him. Initially failing to generate much Japanese interest in his Antarctic venture, he eventually raised enough funds to support a small expedition, which, cheered on by a large crowd, departed in late 1910 with the aim of reaching the Pole the following summer. Pack ice prevented a landing, however, and the men spent the winter in Sydney. By the time they returned south in November 1911, aware that their original aim was now redundant, they focused on undertaking 'as much scientific exploration as practicable'.[31] They were the first humans to stand on Edward VII Land, and sledged southwards for more than 290 km (180 miles) across the Ross Ice Shelf, using teams of Karafuto dogs and moving more quickly than any other expedition at the time.[32] They planted a Japanese flag at their southernmost point – just over 80 degrees – and returned home to an enthusiastic public.

While the crews of the *Fram* and *Kainan-maru* were exchanging visits in the Bay of Whales, Scott's team of five men were hauling their sledges over the polar plateau. They received the message inside Amundsen's tent on 18 January, having reached the Pole the previous day 'under very different circumstances from those expected'.[33] The dawning realization that they would be the second, not the first, team to reach 90 degrees south had been triggered by a flag left at the initial Norwegian camp, a black speck in the distance. 'It is a terrible disappointment, and I am very sorry for my loyal companions', recorded Scott: 'All the day dreams must go; it will be a wearisome return.'[34]

Sir Clements Markham, and Kathleen and Robert Scott on board the *Terra Nova*.

Until he had read Amundsen's telegram in mid-October the previous year, when he was in Melbourne en route to Antarctica, Scott had anticipated his team being alone on the plateau. He knew the possible consequences of the news wired from Norway, writing to his wife Kathleen before he set out on the polar journey: 'If [Amundsen] gets to the Pole, it must be before we do, as he is bound to travel fast with dogs and pretty certain to start early.'[35] Even though Scott's second expedition, like his first, had both scientific and geographic goals, the stakes were high, since the attainment of the Pole had been announced as an explicit aim.

Scott took a tiered approach to the journey, with an advance support team using the new technology of motor-powered sledges setting out with supplies in October 1911, followed by a second group including men, dogs and ponies. These would then be whittled down to a team of four men who would haul sledges along the last leg to the Pole. The use of ponies (a decision influenced by Shackleton's positive reports[36]) meant a later start in the season: the second group departed on the first day of November. From their base at Cape Evans on Ross Island, they planned to cross the Barrier, following the route trail-blazed by Shackleton up the Beardmore Glacier and onto the plateau.

Problems of various kinds – including issues with the motor sledges and the ponies, and difficult snow surfaces – beset the outward journey, but by early January they were on the plateau, fewer than 280 km (150 nautical miles) from the Pole. Scott selected his final team at this point, now deciding on four, rather than three, companions: Wilson, who had accompanied him on his earlier polar trek; Petty Officer Edward 'Taff' Evans, another veteran of the *Discovery* expedition; Lieutenant Henry 'Birdie' Bowers, a naval man who had previously displayed a remarkable imperviousness to the cold; and Lawrence 'Titus' Oates, an army captain. On 4 January the polar party headed south alone.

Postcard from 1912, with image of Captain Scott 'en route to the South Pole'.

"WITH CAPTAIN SCOTT AT THE SOUTH POLE"
Fry's
PURE
Cocoa
& CHOCOLATE
MAKERS TO
H.M. THE KING.

J. S. Fry & Sons Cocoa advertising postcard, *c.* 1910. Fry's Cocoa was one of many commercial sponsors of the *Terra Nova* expedition.

Although the outward trek had had its problems, the decision to continue was not a case of the British choosing lionization over life. They had around a month's rations for the five of them to make the journey to the Pole and back to their depot: 'it ought to see us through'.[37] Fewer than two weeks later, Bowers saw the Norwegians' black flag.

Oates in the stables with some of the Siberian ponies during the *Terra Nova* expedition.

'Great God! this is an awful place', Scott famously wrote in his diary on his first 'night' at the Pole (it was, of course, continually light at this time of year). At lunch the next day, calculating that they were half or three-quarters of a mile from the Pole, they put up their 'poor slighted Union Jack' and took photographs.[38] After a second night they headed back to base, taking the 'ominous black flag' they had originally spotted with them, using its staff as a sail. Scott's journal entry shows the impact on their spirits of their discoveries at the Pole: 'I'm not sure we don't feel the cold more when we stop and camp than we did on the outward march . . . I'm afraid the return journey is going to be dreadfully tiring and monotonous.'[39] It was this, and far more. While they found their food depots, Wilson, Oates and particularly Evans were suffering. Evans had earlier hurt his hand badly while mending a sledge, revealing his injury only when he was in the final team marching towards the Pole. Now it was really beginning to tell, and a concussion sustained in a crevasse encounter made things worse. By early February they were reaching the edge of the plateau, most of them 'fit' but Evans 'going steadily downhill'.[40] By 16 February he had 'nearly broken down in brain', according to Scott; the next day he became delirious, collapsed and lost consciousness, dying in the tent around midnight.[41]

Without Evans, the team was able to move more quickly, but Scott was now worried about the conditions in the late summer season. They were plagued by extreme cold and snow surfaces that made sledging 'like pulling over desert sand, not the least glide in the world'.[42] Soon it was Oates who began to struggle; the harsh conditions had troubled an old war injury to his leg. Scott's diary entries show rising anxiety turning into doubt, by early March, of their chances of 'getting through' while nursing a dying man.[43] Around 16 March Oates famously ended his own suffering, and the team's delay, by walking out of the tent to his death. By now only Scott was keeping a diary, aware that it, rather than the men themselves, would tell the record of their story:

> [Oates] slept through the night before last, hoping not to wake; but he woke in the morning – yesterday. It was blowing a blizzard. He said, 'I am just going outside and may be some time'. He went out into the blizzard and we have not seen him since . . . We knew that poor Oates was walking to his death, but though we tried to dissuade him, we knew it was the act of a brave man and an English gentleman. We all hope to meet the end with a similar spirit, and assuredly the end is not far.[44]

Now desperately short of food and fuel, the three remaining men walked for a few more days, to within 17.5 km (11 miles) of the next depot. Terribly weak, with 'whirling drift' constantly outside their tent, they died, having written farewell letters to their family and friends and, in Scott's case, a compelling 'Message to the Public'.[45] Scott's last diary entry, asking for their families to be looked after, was made on 29 March 1912. It was more than seven months before the diary, in the tent along with the three men's bodies, was found by their traumatized friends. They collapsed the tent over their companions' remains, built a cairn to mark it and returned north. The public did not hear the news until the expedition returned to New Zealand early the following year.

Statue of Robert Falcon Scott in Christchurch, New Zealand (prior to the 2011 earthquake, when the statue was damaged). The statue was sculpted by Scott's widow Kathleen and erected in 1917.

While the quest for the South Pole may have ended on 14 December 1911, no narrative of its exploration ends there: it is not so much Amundsen's victory but the excitement and tragedy of the so-called race to the Pole that has held the popular imagination ever since. It has also generated unending and passionate debate. Even while the British press and public began the inevitable process of mythologizing their polar heroes, questions were asked: about, for example, Scott's organization of the expedition; his selection of four, rather than three, men to accompany him on the run to the Pole; and his decision not to use dogs for the final leg. And while Amundsen's achievement the previous year had been acknowledged and celebrated, even in Britain, issues were raised here, too, especially about the Norwegian's decision to keep his plans a secret.

As the century continued, Scott's reputation in particular was butted and rebutted to the point of tedium, with Roland

Huntford's polemical dual biography *Scott and Amundsen* (1978) being particularly influential. It became obligatory towards the end of the twentieth century to assume that the British leader, far from the heroic martyr celebrated by the British press, was incompetent, underprepared and class-bound; inconsistent and overly sentimental in his attitude towards animals; a poor leader; and suffering from a death wish. In this popular view the explorer was talented only in his ability to write a whitewashing narrative of the journey. Detractors pointed out the numerous mistakes they believed the explorer had made; defenders attempted to explain, contextualize or correct these perceptions in turn. New analyses shed light on controversial points: Susan Solomon in *The Coldest March* (2001), for example, used meteorological data to confirm that the weather on the plateau during Scott's return voyage was, as the team had observed, unusually bad.

Creative writers came into the mix, with the tools at their disposal – multiple perspectives, ambiguity, unreliable narrators – enabling insights and interpretations unavailable to historians. The Norwegian novelist Kåre Holt's *Kappløpet* (The Race, 1974) weaves the two leaders' stories together in alternating chapters; the British writer Beryl Bainbridge's *The Birthday Boys* (1991) deals with Scott's men only, but each member of the polar party narrates in turn. The American author Ursula K. Le Guin changed the focus by publishing an anonymous story, 'Sur', in the *New Yorker* in 1982, the narrator of which claims to have been part of a secret all-women South American expedition that arrived at the Pole before either Scott or Amundsen.

Meanwhile, Scott's journals, appearing in numerous editions and reprints, continued to speak for themselves. When they first appeared in print in 1913 they had been edited, as with the publication of most private journals, and this process became a source of controversy. However, a facsimile of Scott's original entries appeared in the late 1960s, and the whole handwritten account is now available online digitally from the British Library.

Amundsen's account of a seemingly safe and pleasant polar journey was also challenged, although to a lesser degree. Some commentators pointed to his falling out with the experienced but troubled Arctic explorer Hjalmar Johansen: after the first, aborted start for the Pole, Johansen criticized his leader for speeding home ahead of his men, leaving Johansen with no food or tent, and a dangerously frostbitten companion, Kristian Prestrud. Neither man was included in the second polar party; Johansen later committed suicide. Others questioned the treatment of the dogs, some of which were in very poor condition when they were killed. Amundsen himself admitted that the 'over-taxing of these animals' was the 'only dark memory of my stay in the South': the 'daily hard work and the object I would not give up had made me brutal'.[46]

Scott's image looks out from a snow globe purchased from a museum gift shop.

While Amundsen had won the physical 'race to the Pole', then, the moral victory still seemed up for grabs, and it was (and is) quite possible to paint either explorer as hero or villain, by selective inclusion of event and quotation. A recent biographer of Amundsen, Stephen Bown, has put forward a plea for a 'decoupling of these two lives', dismissing the 'so-called race' as 'a literary and historical conceit, contrived at the start by Amundsen and his brother Leon to generate publicity, and perpetuated by authors for nearly a century now, in which Scott's and Amundsen's stories are always told in tandem'. Bown points out that although Amundsen went on to undertake numerous Arctic expeditions and became an international celebrity-explorer, he is nonetheless remembered by posterity largely for his role in the 'race'. The complexity of Scott's character, circumstances and achievement have likewise been flattened for popular consumption into a two-dimensional caricature – a process ironically captured in a recent piece of polar kitsch, a Scott 'snow globe' sold in a museum gift shop as part of the merchandise accompanying a commemorative centenary exhibition. The posthumous fortunes of both men will no doubt continue to wax and wane, with neither able to escape from inevitable comparison with the other.

It was more than 40 years before humans again stood at the South Pole, and they arrived not by dog-sledging or man-hauling but in an R4D-5 U.S. naval aircraft. The Pole had not remained entirely in peace throughout this time, however. 'Heroic Era' explorers had recognized the potential of flight in the region, with Scott launching an air balloon during the *Discovery* expedition, from which Shackleton took photographs, and Mawson purchasing an aeroplane for his Australasian Antarctic Expedition. Neither effort went very well, but by the 1920s other explorers were taking up the challenge, and another 'race to the Pole' was in the making.

The Australian explorer Hubert Wilkins, famous for his aviation exploits in the Arctic and elsewhere, secured funding to attempt Antarctic flights from the publishing magnate William Randolph Hearst, who offered a $10,000 bonus if Wilkins reached the South Pole. Wilkins's main focus, however, was on a different part of the continent.[47] In late 1928 he and his co-pilot Ben Eielson made the first flight in the Antarctic,

Scott's polar party's famous 'selfie', now on a coffee mug.

In the early 1930s Parker Bros. Inc. released this board game based on Byrd's first Antarctic expedition.

from Deception Island, off the Antarctic Peninsula. Soon after they flew over Graham Land, reaching over 71 degrees south before turning back.

The American naval officer Richard Byrd, having heard about the bonus Hearst had promised Wilkins, was worried that the Australian might steal his thunder: 'You must not forget that Wilkins is out to lick us', he told his fund manager.[48] Around the time that Wilkins made his first Antarctic flight, Byrd's expedition arrived at the Ross Ice Shelf, establishing a base in the ice, 'Little America'. Byrd was another Pole-hunter. He was already famous for his North Pole overflight of 1926, although the validity of his claim has been contested ever since. Amundsen flew over the North Pole in an airship just a few days later; thus, given that Cook's and Peary's claims have also been discredited, he may actually have achieved his childhood dream of being the first to reach (or at least fly above) the spot. On Byrd's return, the Norwegian veteran asked the American explorer about his next goal, and received the reply – only half-joking – 'The South Pole'.[49]

This was more easily said than done. Among other challenges, Byrd's plane (a Ford Trimotor) needed to negotiate a mountain range and, unable to gain sufficient altitude to pass over it, had to fly up a glacier between the peaks. The plane took off in late November 1929, carrying a four-man team, including Byrd himself as navigator. To clear the pass they had to dump emergency food bags, and even then they made it by only a few hundred feet. They flew over the Pole in the early hours of the morning (darkness, of course, was not a problem), dropped an American flag and returned to base along Amundsen's route, arriving around eighteen hours after they departed. The expedition had an enthusiastic welcome when it arrived back in the United States in 1929, with a documentary film of the achievement, *With Byrd to the South Pole*, released the following year.

No further attempt to reach the South Pole by land was made until early 1958, when Sir Edmund Hillary led a team of three tractors across from Ross Island. Hillary had not actually planned to reach the Pole: as part of the Commonwealth Trans-Antarctic Expedition, he was laying depots for another party led by the British geologist and explorer Vivian Fuchs, which was

Snowcat crossing a crevasse during the Commonweath Trans-Antarctic Expedition (1955–8).

Swedish poster (1930) by Erik Rohman, promoting Byrd's expedition film.

travelling from the Weddell Sea in motorized vehicles. Having laid his last depot 500 miles from the Pole, and with Fuchs delayed by the difficult terrain, Hillary – who had already hunted the 'third Pole' (Mount Everest) successfully four years earlier – decided to push on, arriving more than two weeks earlier than the other team. While Fuchs, the overall leader and instigator of the expedition, went on to complete the continental crossing a couple of months later, he was understandably put out.

Hillary's arrival at 90 degrees, although an impressive achievement duly celebrated in the press, was very different from Amundsen's. The New Zealander was 'led off by friendly hands towards the warmth and fresh food of the Pole Station'.[50] The empty plateau was now occupied by prefabricated buildings and ex-Korean War Jamesway huts, inhabited by a community of eighteen men. The Pole itself was surrounded by a circle of empty fuel drums. He had arrived at the end of the Earth and found a U.S. military base.

5 Settling in at 'Ninety South'

It is one thing to *reach* the South Pole: to spend a day or two locating the spot, planting a flag and celebrating your arrival, before returning home again. But what does it mean to *live* there, when the excitement of conquest flattens out into the mundanity of occupation? 'Living at the South Pole would have been the highpoint of my life', mused the sick and aging Richard Byrd in 1956 about the place he had flown over almost three decades earlier.[1] But could day-to-day existence really rival the glamour of first arrival?

Kim Stanley Robinson's near-future science-fiction novel *Antarctica* (1997) includes a telling episode set at the Pole. It centres on the character of Wade Norton, a political adviser to a Washington senator. Arriving at 90 degrees south in a Hercules, Wade concludes – once the initial shock and excitement have worn off – that 'The South Pole was not a place where there was much to do.' Wandering around the buildings, he considers it

> all very interesting; but not. Only the idea that all these rooms were at the South Pole made them other than a weird cross of military base, airport lounge, lab lounge, and motel. It was, to his surprise, extremely boring; boring in a way that contrasted very strongly to his experience in Antarctica so far.[2]

Robinson's character does not, however, *live* at the South Pole – he is on a brief visit, fact-gathering for his employer, and as he discovers, the locals' experiences of the place are quite different from his.

'The funny thing about the Pole', writes Jerri Nielsen in her account of a winter spent as a doctor at the station, 'was how quickly you came to accept it as your home.'[3] Those who live there for months or years know the South Pole as the site of a community with its own subcultures, vocabulary, points of etiquette, social hierarchies, pleasures and frustrations. 'Polies' drop the article that outsiders use and refer more familiarly to being 'at Pole', or going 'to Pole'. As one writer observes, 'Pole is a specific place, a territory where people live and work; the South Pole, although it's only a few hundred yards away and can be fixed by GPS, is more an idea, a geophysical ideal.'[4] The isolation of the community – and perhaps also the cachet of living at the end of the Earth – creates an intense bond among its residents. 'When visiting Pole from McMurdo', suggests Nicholas Johnson in his irreverent insider's account of the U.S. Antarctic Program, 'it is good to have a reference. If one is introduced by a Polie, Pole is generally a friendlier, less cliquish, and more inclusive community than McMurdo. Otherwise, who knows.'[5]

The South Pole could claim locals for the first time in 1957, when eighteen men (scientists and naval personnel) and a young dog spent most of the year there. During the International Geophysical Year – a coordinated scientific effort running for eighteen months from mid-1957 – twelve nations established more than 50 stations in the Antarctic, including a United States base on the Geographic Pole itself. Unsurprisingly, its construction presented considerable logistical and physical challenges. Late in 1956 airforce planes dropped supplies, equipment, fuel, timber and prefabricated buildings by parachute to a small but hardy group of naval construction workers below. The men initially lived in tents and then in Jamesway huts – canvas-covered structures originally designed for use in the Korean War. Things did not always go to plan: parachutes failed, oil leaked, tomato juice splattered all over the snow and a set of the *Encyclopaedia Britannica* plummeted deep into it, never to be seen again.[6] But in late January 1957 the station was ready for the eighteen winterovers, who would finish off the job when they moved in. At the larger American station on Ross Island, McMurdo, an official opening ceremony was held – unbeknown to the personnel at the Pole – complete with speeches, marines in full dress and messages from President Eisenhower and various other dignitaries. The station was officially named 'Amundsen-Scott IGY South Pole Station' (when settlement continued beyond 1958, the 'IGY' was dropped).[7]

The infrastructure was comparatively basic: the buildings were constructed from modular panels of aluminium and plywood. There were no windows except triple-glazed skylights – snow would cover the buildings 'up to the eaves' over winter.[8] The complex included a garage, powerhouse and water supply building; a building for inflating and launching weather balloons; a radio and meteorological shack topped by a dome designed for the radar tracking of the balloons; a tower for auroral observations; a science building; an astronomical observatory; a photo lab; a toilet; sleeping quarters (in the Jamesways); a recreation room; and a mess hall. Field telephones linked the various areas, and the buildings were physically connected by tunnels, which were also used to store fuel and supplies, but were not heated. The scientific leader, Paul Siple, predicting temperatures down to −50°C (−60°F) in the tunnels during the winter, worried about their utility: 'Every time we leave our quarters to eat, work, wash, see a movie, or get a midnight snack, we shall have to dress to the teeth.'[9] A separate building some distance away would provide emergency shelter and supplies in the case of fire.

For Siple, who had wintered in Antarctica several times before – initially as a nineteen-year-old Boy Scout with Byrd's first expedition – conditions were comparatively luxurious: 'Antarctic living is changing . . . It seems a bit strange to have hot water, warm latrines, shower baths, clothes-washing machines, and even electric sunlamps . . . It is wonderful, too, to be able to talk [by radio-phone] occasionally with our families back in the States.'[10] They also used the radio occasionally to talk to celebrities (such as Dean Martin). Domestic issues took on a larger than usual significance in the isolated and extreme environment:

a shortage of tobacco had the men ransacking bins for butts; a problem with cakes not rising was referred to the cake-mix company in Minneapolis, which advised on adjustments to be made at high altitude; and the temperature of the toilet seats, 4°C (40°F), was a source of considerable stress until the physician found a way to produce the 'warm latrines' of Siple's description (he simply added a hinged plywood lid beneath the seat to insulate it from the sewage pit formed in the ice).[11] The men worked long hours but rested on Sundays; a church service would be held after supper. Entertainment over the dark winter consisted of music, films several times a week, conversations, ham-radio sessions, regular lectures and occasional bingo.[12]

Living at the Pole presented the men with unusual difficulties when it came to orienting themselves in space and time. Since the lines of longitude, which are conventionally used to define time differences, come together at the Pole, any time zone can effectively be selected. The station personnel enjoyed the joke that by walking in a small circle around the Pole, they could technically move ahead a day. Siple originally opted to set South Pole time at Greenwich Mean Time, but for ease of radio communication eventually decided on adopting the same time used at McMurdo – which in turn adopted the time zone used by New Zealand, the base for the navy flights to the Ross Sea. Direction posed another problem. At the Geographic Pole itself, whichever way you face is obviously north. They prevented confusion by 'arbitrarily superimposing a standard Mercator projection over the top of the polar map', with Greenwich 'North' and the Ross Sea area 'South'.[13]

The Pole itself was originally represented symbolically by a striped bamboo pole, topped by a mirrored glass ball and supporting an American flag, which stood on the roof of the garage. Later, when the winterovers had more accurately located the Pole, the point was marked by both the American and United Nations flags, and surrounded by a circle of empty oil drums. After the sun returned, some of the men, restless now that their stay was drawing to a close, made an unsuccessful search for another polar marker: Amundsen's buried tent.[14]

Entrance to the Dome Station in 1981.

The first winterovers departed towards the end of the year as another group moved in. The station, which was not intended as a permanent structure, housed its small, constantly refreshed community for almost another twenty years. Numerous additions and changes were made to meet new needs and deal with the inevitably deteriorating buildings, but by the late 1960s the station was covered by 10 m (33 ft) of snow and badly in need of replacement.[15] The National Science Foundation, working with the U.S. Navy, decided on a geodesic dome as the best achievable design. Naval crews constructed the new station over three consecutive summers. Around 50 m (165 ft) wide at its base on the ice, 16 m (50 ft) high, and accessed via a tunnel, the aluminium dome contained three double-storey prefabricated buildings. Itself unheated, and mostly covered with snow during the winter, the dome functioned as an 'elaborate windbreak that protected the heated buildings inside'.[16] The new facility accommodated

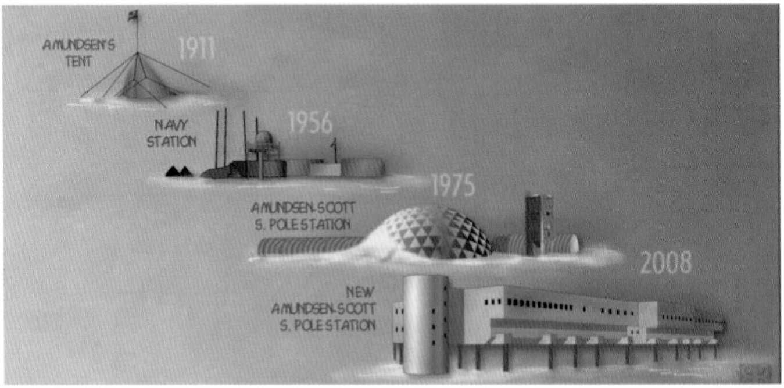

Timeline of the evolution of South Pole Station.

only a handful more people than its predecessor had, but offered more spacious living conditions and far more amenities. Later, huts and tents outside became an additional 'summer camp', and there were also separate buildings for medical, scientific and other equipment, some connected by tunnels to the dome.[17]

Opening in early 1975, and operating under the auspices of the National Science Foundation rather than the Navy, the dome functioned for more than 30 years, increasingly encroached by the surrounding snow. Over the years new buildings and equipment were added as scientific and personnel requirements changed. Nielsen describes the dome as it was in 1999:

> The galley, to the right of the entrance, was the first building. It was just like a Navy ship's galley, no surprise, since the Seabees had built it in the 1970s. The kitchen and dining room were on the lower level, with a smaller dining area upstairs, and the 90 South Bar. Unlike American oil rigs and aircraft carriers, this ship was not dry. Smoking and drinking were permitted at the bar, on a bring-your-own basis. Predictably, the galley and the bar were the focus of social life at the Pole.
>
> Separate from the galley but accessible from a second-floor walkway, was the 'freshie shack,' a building heated to the temperature of a household refrigerator and used for storing vegetables and other DNF (do not freeze) items, such as beer and soda pop. The next building housed the communication center on the ground floor, and the library, pool room, offices,

> and South Pole store on the top level. The third and largest prefab structure held the computer lab, the science office, and on the top floor, dormitory rooms and the sauna. A berthing annex had been attached to this building to house still more people. A hydroponic greenhouse (with artificial lighting) rested on its roof.[18]

Power was produced from generators turned by diesel engines burning aviation fuel. To keep the buildings within the dome (comparatively) warm, coolant heated by the engines was piped in and returned, cooled, to the engines.[19] By this stage, a device known as a 'Rodriguez well' or 'rodwell' was (and still is) used to create caverns of melted water deep under the ice, which was pumped to the station. Because of the energy needed to melt the ice (it never rains at the Pole), water usage is severely limited: Polies are allowed a two-minute shower twice a week, and a load of laundry once a week. All waste is removed to McMurdo and thence out of Antarctica, except human excrement, which runs through metal corridors to form a frozen sewage bulb beneath the ice, in the space created by an old rodwell.

Like its predecessor, the Dome Station eventually outlived its usefulness: the snow that accumulated around it caused structural problems, and it could not deal with the increasing demand for accommodation. Construction of a third station – with all materials brought in by Hercules aircraft – was approved in 1997 and completed more than ten years later. Around the same time,

Waste containers at Amundsen-Scott South Pole Station, a couple of days before sunset, 2013.

a controversial 'road' – a smoothed-out snow surface, with crevasses filled in with ice – was constructed and maintained between McMurdo and the South Pole, meaning fuel and supplies could be brought in overland by tractor-train.

The new station design needed to deal better with the problems that plagued the site, particularly the pile-up of snow against buildings due to wind. The solution was an elevated building sitting on pylons: the shape of the building – like the wing of a plane – directs strong wind through the pylons to scour away piled snow as much as possible. In the future, the whole building can be 'jacked up' above the accumulated snow if necessary. This new, elevated station can house 150 people during summer, and enables personnel to reach accommodation, recreation and work spaces without having to brave the cold. Unlike the previous two stations, this one has windows, allowing its occupants natural light and views of the plateau on which they live. Following the completion of the new station, its two earlier incarnations were destroyed: the Dome was removed, with its top section preserved in a museum in California, and the buried Navy station, now potentially dangerous to vehicles on the surface of the ice, was demolished.

U.S. Antarctic Program personnel pose in front of the final panels of the dismantled geodesic dome, January 2010.

Amundsen-Scott South Pole Station, 2012.

The new Pole station has attracted the moniker 'The South Pole Hotel', which captures the combination of increasing luxury with what for some of its occupants is a clinical, impersonal feel. The visual artist Connie Samaras, who visited the continent with the U.S. Antarctic Artists and Writers Program in 2004, observes that

> The interior itself feels like a cross between interchangeable non-places like LAX and Southern California shopping malls, mixed with a set design for a *Star Trek* episode. Both the design and the construction materials, particularly in the sleeping areas, are engineered to repel personal touches. In contrast to the Dome, the design of the Amundsen-Scott berths resolutely conveys that all traces of a given occupant will automatically be disappeared once she or he leaves the quarters with only the timeless presence of the building remaining.[20]

That the station seems to be like a combination of 'stealth bomber' and hotel seems 'hardly ironic' to Samaras, who notes the running of the station by Raytheon, a multi-billion-dollar American defence contractor, and the outsourcing of catering

Women arrive at the South Pole for the first time in 1969.

(while Samaras was there) to the Marriott corporation. Kim Stanley Robinson's vision of a station that looks like a 'spaceliner' and feels like 'a weird cross of military base, airport lounge, lab lounge, and motel' appears to have come to fruition.[21]

While the infrastructure at the Pole was evolving over its 50 years of human settlement, so was its human community. The first group of eighteen winterovers were remarkably homogeneous. Siple recounts that the men 'were an average cross section of Americans descended from a wide variety of European stock'. None of the crew was Hispanic or African American, and – having been tested for 'manly interests and qualities' – they were all 'he-men', a term that for Siple suggests unquestionable heterosexuality as well as physical hardihood. The men maintained an unforgiving culture of toughness by 'riding' any of their fellows who were seen to be shirking their work or showing weakness, paying no attention to mitigating circumstances, such as injury and sickness.[22] While the Russian IGY effort included women researchers on Antarctic vessels, none wintered on the continent. U.S. policy excluded women at both McMurdo and South Pole stations for over a decade: the first women arrived at the South Pole in 1969, a group of six famously stepping arm-in-arm from the plane ramp together, meaning that none had precedence. They were all researchers working elsewhere on the continent; their very brief visit was 'something of a public relations exercise', but symbolically significant nonetheless.[23] The first time women worked at the South Pole was in 1973, with the first winterover occurring in 1979.

By the turn of the twenty-first century, the South Pole community had become more diverse. Veteran Polie Bill Spindler's unofficial website devoted to the history of the place provides a detailed account of the changing make-up of wintering personnel, who as of 2015 totalled nearly 1,500 during the whole period of human inhabitation of the Pole – more than 200 of them women. These days there are normally about 50 residents in any one winter, and it is not unusual for one-quarter of them to be women. National and racial diversity have also expanded over the half-century of human occupation of the Pole: to Spindler's best knowledge, the first time a Hispanic man wintered was in 1961, and an African American in 1969. The first non-American citizen to winter was a Japanese scientist in 1960, and over the following decades citizens of over twenty different nations have made up the wintering community. The age range of winter-overs has also expanded to include people in their sixties and seventies.[24] This diversification is relative, however. Newcomers to the station can still be struck by its homogeneity: 'Coming from Southern California, it was shocking to be in a population, scientists and personnel, where there were hardly any people of color and where, like the '50s in the U.S., it was somehow acceptable.'[25]

While the station community has grown in numbers and (to some extent) diversity over the last 50 years, there are inevitably home-grown processes of inclusivity and exclusivity that operate. The formation of cliques and the inevitable forces of peer pressure can make life intense in such a small and isolated community, and for those who do not fit in the only place to escape is into themselves. Especially during the period after midwinter, when the novelty is wearing off but the long, dark winter continues, expeditioners can become withdrawn and behave eccentrically – they are, to use U.S. Antarctic jargon, 'toast'.[26] Individual projects, such as craft, become important ways of maintaining equilibrium. The personality of the station manager can have a significant impact on the experience for all involved. As at many other Antarctic stations, there is a social divide between scientists ('beakers') and support personnel. (In the winter, the ratio of these groups changes: scientific personnel drop to a skeleton staff and the majority of staff are technicians and tradespeople involved in the running of the station and its equipment.)

Similar to other Antarctic stations, a hierarchy of 'ice time' prevails, in which a stay during winter is more impressive than a summer, and returning for multiple seasons is more impressive still. The South Pole trumps other locations on this scale:

> If you've done multiple winters, you haven't been to Pole. If you've done a summer at Pole, you haven't done a winter at Pole. If you've done a winter at Pole, you haven't done multiple winters at Pole. And, finally, once you've done multiple winters at Pole, you are afraid to leave Antarctica because you'll have to pay for food and look both ways before crossing the street.[27]

There are a surprising number of people in the last category: in 2015 nine of the 45 winterovers had wintered before once or more, and two were in their eleventh winter.[28]

Wintering staff are systematically vetted for suitability. Even if you have the necessary qualifications or experience, ongoing health problems can easily rule you out. Statistically speaking the South Pole is not a particularly dangerous place – there have been six deaths in the 50 years of settlement, three of which were extreme tourists: skydivers whose parachutes did not deploy. These figures, however, belie the challenging nature of the environment. Apart from the unthinkable cold, the elevation above sea level creates problems, with many newcomers suffering symptoms of altitude sickness and residents experiencing ongoing issues due to the lower levels of atmospheric oxygen. The long periods of daylight and darkness also have a physiological impact, and the dry air causes skin problems.[29] Since planes cannot land during the winter months, any illnesses or accidents can only be treated by the one doctor present. All winterovers are given medical screenings, but emergencies nonetheless occur, most famously Nielsen's self-diagnosis of breast cancer, which required her to take her own tissue samples and treat herself with chemotherapy drugs airdropped to the base, before being evacuated on an earlier (and hence riskier) than usual flight.

The small, isolated, claustrophobic community and the dark, freezing winter also represent psychological challenges. The first group of winterovers were subject to 'extensive psychological testing' prior to selection, to exclude those with 'claustrophobia or mental disorders' and to gauge their 'manly interests and qualities'. Siple asserts that Antarctic conditions reveal a person's core characteristics: 'Whatever a man was inherently would be intensified during the close-quarters winter night. A mean man would grow meaner; a kind man would grow kinder.' While this is not self-evident – why should a person's behaviour under extreme and highly artificial circumstances be considered their 'true self'? – it voices a common maxim of Antarctic expeditioners. Having passed prior screening, the first eighteen wintering men were required to take repeated psychological questionnaires while at the Pole to supply data on isolated living. One divisive exercise, which asked them to list those in their community they

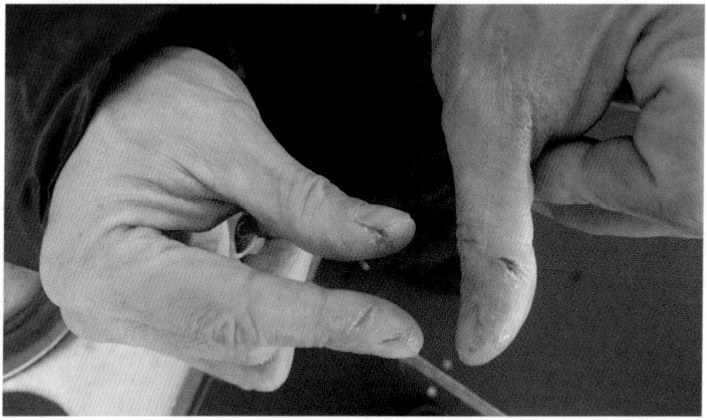

Antarctica's dry, cold environment can make ordinary tasks more difficult.

disliked, giving reasons for their antipathy, created so much resistance that it was abandoned.[30] More recent winterovers are also required to take psychological tests in advance. Nielsen writes that recruiters 'were looking for people who were stable, easy to get along with, and intuitive . . . They wanted to weed out people with personality disorders, chronic complainers, the chronically depressed, substance abusers, and who knows what else.'[31]

For psychologists, the small wintering community at the Pole provides a unique opportunity to study group dynamics. From the early years of the first station, researchers have examined the challenges 'encountered by a collection of heterogeneous strangers in developing a distinct microculture adapted to this unusual human situation'.[32] One study, conducted over three years in the 1990s, looked at the formation of different social patterns in successive wintering crews, noting that the least functional group had the strongest clique structure.[33] Research on both group and individual psychology provides data that can be fed back into the selection processes for wintering personnel and also informs organizations such as NASA that are interested in the similarly confined and extreme conditions of space exploration.

One significant change to the isolation of the South Polar community in recent years is the increase in communication with the world 'back home'. Polies today have fairly regular access to email, Internet and phone – subject, admittedly, to the availability of communication satellites, which are far less accessible near the poles. Many maintain blogs outlining their Antarctic experiences and displaying their photographic efforts. Siple's companions, relying on the occasional use of radio, had far fewer chances to unload frustrations and share problems with family and friends. Worrying about the men's lack of 'an emotional outlet', Siple thought it wise to have a dog – Bravo, a young Alaskan Malamute born in Antarctica – stay with them over winter as a non-judgemental and discreet listener, although in the end the puppy bonded closely to a single man.[34] Contemporary technology makes confidants far more readily available to Polies, although it also means that the demands and stresses of life at home can impinge on the supposedly isolated South Pole experience; for Nielsen, emails and Internet phones were a 'mixed blessing'.[35]

One aspect of wintering that has remained steady since the Pole was settled is the need for ritual and periodic celebration in order to punctuate otherwise depressingly homogenous periods of time and to provide events around which the community can cohere. Antarctic expeditioners have long recognized the wisdom of this: Douglas Mawson, leader of a group of men living on the coast of Antarctica in the winters of 1912 and 1913, recalled that 'the mania for celebration became so great that reference was frequently made to the almanac. During one featureless interval, the anniversary of the First Lighting of London by Gas was observed with extraordinary *éclat*.'[36] At the South Pole, where extremes of temperature and darkness are much more pronounced than at the continent's edge, the need to incorporate ritualized festivity is even greater. Siple's men celebrated the winter solstice – the midpoint of the long polar night

The absence of trees does not stop South Pole personnel from celebrating Christmas.

– with a 'gala celebration' involving a candelabra constructed from pipe fittings, home-made firecrackers and champagne toasts.[37] Other 'holidays' were declared for the monthly full moon, lunar eclipses and birthdays.

Over the following half-century the importance of rituals and celebrations to mark important points in the South Polar year has not abated. Midwinter continues to be a significant event in the polar calendar, marked by a series of established elements, such as (for a number of years) a special airdrop, with gifts from the previous winterovers; a lavish meal and new supplies; formal dress or costumes; elaborate menus and decorations; theatricals, concerts or dancing; greetings from other Antarctic bases and government dignitaries; and an ironic screening of the horror film *The Shining* (in which the caretaker of an isolated, snowed-in hotel runs amok with an axe). Another significant time is the farewelling of the summer personnel. John Carpenter's Antarctic horror film *The Thing* is a favourite for marking the departure of the last plane, which leaves the winterovers, like the film's doomed expeditioners, completely isolated. Far from horror, their response to abandonment is often euphoria, with space and resources now freed up, and the much-anticipated adventure of wintering finally begun. (Conversely, at the other end of the season, the arrival of incoming expeditioners – intruders into the insular community – can create tensions among 'toasty' winterovers.) More familiar significant dates are marked in specific ways at the Pole: on New Year's Day, the placing of the new Geographic Pole marker; and at Christmas the annual 'Race Around the World', which takes competitors (most running or walking, some in vehicles) around a course – varying from year to year but usually around 3.2 km (2 miles) long – that passes through every time zone. Another well-known tradition is the '300 Club': when the temperature drops below −73°C (−100°F), initiates clad in boots and little else sit in a +90°C (+200°F) sauna for as long as possible before dashing outside, ideally to the Ceremonial Pole and back again. And in addition to these regularly repeated rituals, there are occasionally more official ceremonies: the first of several weddings at the South Pole took place in 1985.[38]

Traditions, rituals and ceremonies provide the ever-changing South Polar community with a sense of stability and permanence. But despite the presence of veterans of numerous winters, is it ever really possible to put down 'roots' in the shifting icescape? With no one ever born or buried in the place, no families or children, no retired people, no planting of trees or gardens (with the exception of hydroponics) and all resources flown in from outside, has humanity really *settled* the South Pole? While humans have done their best to settle in – to establish an ongoing presence, construct sophisticated ways of making life tolerable and develop a relationship with place through tradition and ritual – they are, and for the foreseeable future will remain, sojourners at 90 degrees south.

6 Highest, Coldest, Driest . . . ?

What kind of place, physically speaking, had humanity colonized when it began building the first scientific station at the South Pole? Any description of Antarctica's physical conditions is inevitably drawn towards a familiar list of superlatives: it is famously the highest, coldest, driest continent, not to mention the iciest, windiest and emptiest. This cliché is difficult to avoid in descriptions of the Antarctic environment – especially when it comes to the South Pole, instinctively conceived as the most extreme point in this extreme continent. But how well do these adjectives really apply to the Pole?

It is impossible, of course, to separate the natural environment of the Pole from the continent that surrounds it: an inconceivable 26.5 million cubic km (6.4 million cubic miles) of ice slowly sliding over bedrock. A good deal of this bedrock is below sea level, partly due to the immense weight of the ice. If the ice melted away, the bedrock would eventually spring up (a process called 'isostatic rebound'), but some of it would still remain underwater. Beneath the ice are substantial subglacial lakes – more than 300 have been discovered thus far – with the largest, Lake Vostok, about twice the volume of Lake Victoria. The ice sheets sit on a layer of liquid water, created by the friction of the ice moving over rock, combined with geothermal energy.[1] Attached to the 'grounded' ice are floating ice shelves, including the massive Ross and Ronne-Filchner shelves which make almost an extra million cubic kilometres of ice. The continent, ice shelves and islands included, has an area about 1.4 times that of the

U.S.; less than half of 1 per cent is free of ice. Antarctica is divided into two regions by the aptly named Transantarctic mountain range, more than 3,200 km (2,000 miles) long: West Antarctica, which includes the Antarctic Peninsula; and the significantly higher, colder and larger East Antarctica. The Pole sits not far into East Antarctica, where the ice sheet slopes gradually up towards its high domes further into the interior.

In H. P. Lovecraft's novella *At the Mountains of Madness* (1936), a scientific expedition comes to grief while investigating an Antarctic range soaring up well above the height of Everest; reality, however, is more mundane. The Transantarctic Mountains are impressive, but nothing like the height of the Himalayas or the Andes. Antarctica's highest peak, Mount Vinson, is found in another of the continent's mountain ranges, the Ellsworth Mountains in West Antarctica, running perpendicular to the Transantarctics. (A third major chain runs along the Antarctic Peninsula.[2]) At around 4,900 m (16,000 ft), Mount Vinson is just a little higher than Mount Blanc. It is not the mountains but the height of the icecap itself that pushes Antarctica's mean height – about 2,200 m (7,200 ft), excluding floating ice shelves – to

Illustration of a cross-section of Lake Vostok, the largest known subglacial lake.

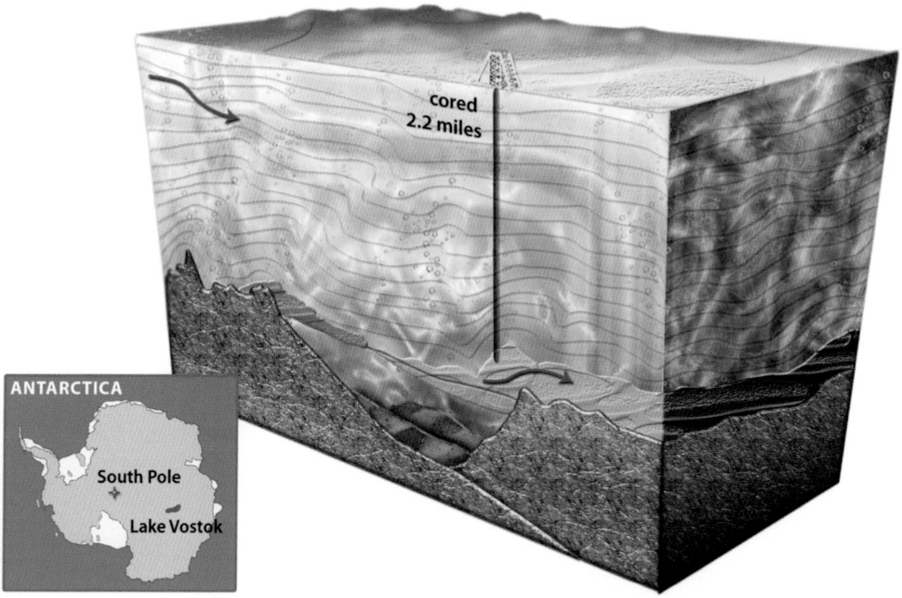

Peaks in the Transantarctic Mountains.

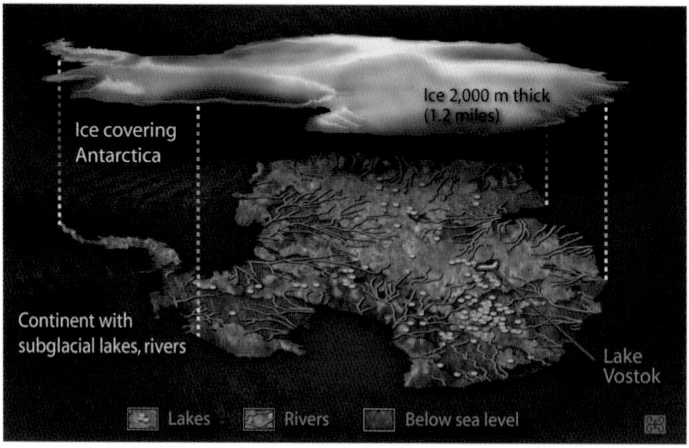

Illustration of the aquatic system believed to be beneath the Antarctic ice sheet.

more than twice that of the world's continental average. The highest part of the ice sheet is Dome A, an elevated plain sitting at approximately 4,100 m (13,200 ft). The Pole, lying on the plateau's sloping edge, is much lower, about 2,800 m (9,300 ft) above sea level.

High means cold: the Russian station Vostok, at around 3,500 m (11,500 ft) above sea level, has recorded the coldest air temperature in the continent and the world (−89.2°C/−128.6°F). Dome A, the site of the Chinese base Kunlun, has the unenviable honour of the lowest *average* temperature: slightly below −58°C (−72°F), about 5°C colder than Vostok's average. It may

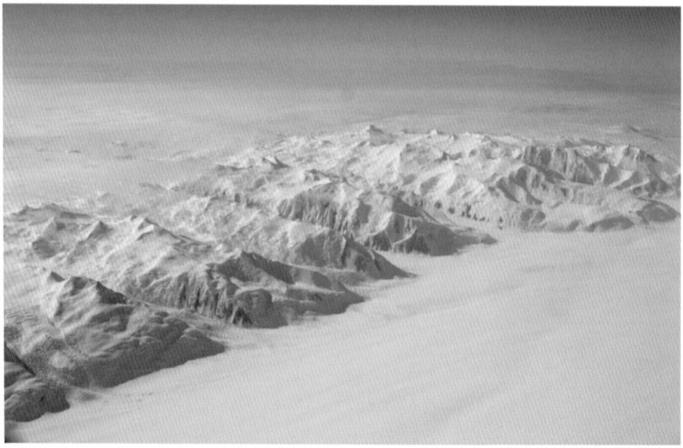

Aerial shot of the Transantarctic Mountains.

Boiling water thrown into the air by a winterover flash-freezes at -68° C (-90° F).

soon take the lead for the absolute low now that a year-round weather station is in place. The Pole is milder by the standards of the plateau: –49.4°C (–56.9°F) on average, with a record low of -82.8°C (–117°F) in 1982 and a high of –12.3°C (–9.9°F) in 2011.[3] Much nearer the coast of the continent and on the Antarctic Peninsula highs can easily reach positive figures: 15°C (59°F) is the upper record. Of course, the plateau's cold temperature is not only due to its height, but to the low angle of the sun's rays and the reflection of sunlight off the ice – the same factors behind the cold temperatures of the Arctic. Another reason, besides height, that Antarctica is the colder of the two regions is its isolation: it lies a long way from any other continent and is surrounded by the cold circumpolar current.

Cold, in turn, means dry. Very low temperatures, together with sinking air above, result in very low precipitation: around 13 cm (5 in.) a year on average for Antarctica, well under the 25-cm (10-in.) mark below which an environment, as a rule of thumb, is classed as a desert.[4] The high inland areas of East Antarctica are even drier: just over three-quarters of an inch (2 cm) at Dome A, and around 7 cm (3 in.) at the Pole (snow accumulation can be higher or lower than actual precipitation in a particular place because of windblown snow).[5] While there are particular regions on Earth that are far drier (for example, parts of the Atacama desert in South America – also a high place), no continent is so dry on average. Although it does rain in warmer coastal areas of the continent, most of the precipitation in the Antarctic interior takes the form of snow grains and 'diamond dust' – ice crystals falling from a clear sky. Since snow does not melt in the continent's

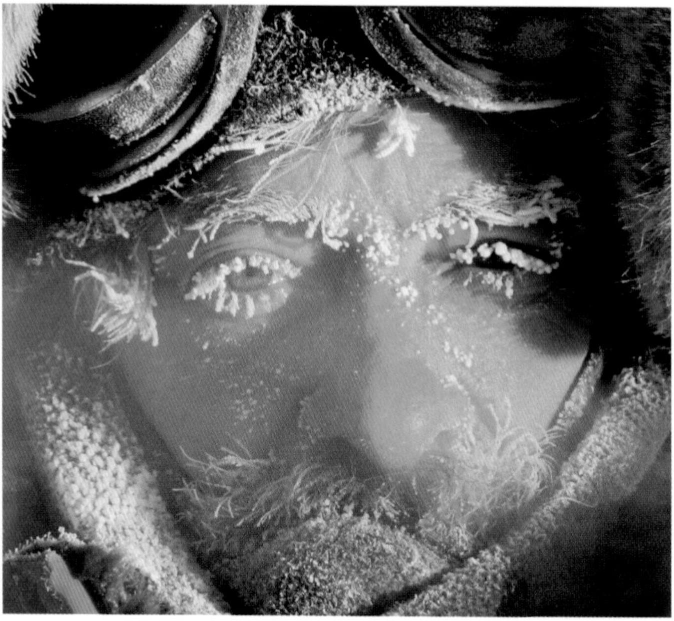

Frosted face at -62° C (-80° F).

interior, after millions of years it builds up to create the stupendous ice sheets evident today.

Only a contrarian would contest Antarctica's claim to being the iciest place on Earth: the mean thickness of the ice (excluding the floating ice shelves) is around 2,100 m (7,000 ft). Intuitively you would think that the highest place would also boast the thickest ice, but this assumption ignores the shape of the bedrock beneath the ice, itself pushed down by the huge weight on top of it. At the Byrd Glacier in West Antarctica, it dips down to almost 2,900 m (9,500 ft) below sea level, whereas the Pole's bedrock is close to sea level. Elsewhere, the bedrock is elevated, varying from around 950–2,450 m (3,100 to 8,000 ft) under Dome A, for example. This means that although this is the highest part of the ice sheet, it does not sit on the most ice: the layer under Dome A averages around 2,200 m (7,300 ft), considerably less than the ice underneath the Pole, although it rises to more than 3,000 m (10,000 ft) at its thickest, the site of Kunlun Station.[6] The continent's thickest ice can be found an impressive 4,776 m (15,669 ft) above the Astrolabe Subglacial

A helicopter is used to collect data on the sea ice below

Basin, a small wedge of East Antarctica claimed by France. The depth of ice, and the varied nature of the bedrock, means that topological features that would dominate other landscapes are entirely hidden: under the ice of East Antarctica lie the Gamburtsev Mountains, a range similar in size to the European Alps (hence the remarkably varied height of the bedrock under Dome A). Occasionally, peaks will jut out of the ice sheet – these are called 'nunataks', an Inuit term transplanted from the Arctic. Of course, continental ice is only one part of the story: Antarctica is also surrounded by sea ice, seasonally expanding and shrinking from around 2 million square km (770,000 square miles) in the southern hemisphere's autumn to 15 million square km (5.8 million square miles) in the spring.[7]

Wind speed is also determined by the continent's topology. The strongest winds are the 'katabatics', formed when cold and

therefore dense air flows off the plateau under the force of gravity and accelerates down the steep slopes near the coast. Douglas Mawson, leading an expedition based at Cape Denison on the coast of East Antarctica in the early twentieth century, believed he was at the 'Home of the Blizzard', and he was not wrong: Cape Denison is not just the windiest place in the Antarctic, it is the windiest on the planet, at surface level. During the two years Mawson stayed there, the average wind speed was around 71 kph (44 mph). The highest wind speed ever recorded on the continent, however, was a couple of hundred miles away at Dumont d'Urville Station: 327 kph (199 mph). Well over the speed required for a Category 5 hurricane, it is also the equal highest wind speed recorded in the world (the other was at Mount Washington in New Hampshire).[8] The top wind speed at the Pole, sitting on only a slight slope in the continent's interior, is 93 kph (58 mph); average wind speed is about 15 kph (9 mph), technically a gentle breeze.[9]

All these extremes mean that Antarctica is by far the emptiest continent, with no indigenous people, no permanent inhabitants and a temporary population varying from about 1,000 in winter to more than four times that in summer, excluding tourists. So far, fewer than a dozen people have been born on the continent, all at Chilean and Argentinian stations, which also maintain schools. The population of the Pole ranges from around 50 in the winter to well over 200 in the summer. It is by no means the smallest station and not necessarily the most isolated. Several inland stations might make the latter claim, depending on the criteria used. The uninhabited South Pole of Inaccessibility is one possible benchmark for the most isolated point on the continent. Isolated population bases include Kunlun Station on Dome A – but this runs only in the summer – and the Russian year-round station Vostok, which has a wintering population of not much more than a dozen. Of course, temporary field bases may be smaller and more isolated than these stations.

The Pole, then, is extreme, but not quite as extreme in any one measure as other places in the continent. It can, of course, claim the longest continuous period of darkness (and light) –

previous: Sea ice breaking up in Terra Nova Bay.

Antarctica is the windiest of all Earth's continents.

half a year – although it shares this record with its northern counterpart. Ultimately, it seems that the Pole's primary claim to fame, in terms of geographic and climatic extremes, is that it is, by definition, the most southerly point on the planet.

What is there to see at the Pole, human infrastructure aside? For most people, the name 'South Pole' probably conjures up a wide, icy plain – an image characterized more than anything else by absence. 'It just looks flat, greyish, and, frankly, rather dull', observes the science journalist Gabrielle Walker, speaking about the East Antarctic ice sheet. She is describing a view from an aircraft, however. While at surface level the plateau is not

Yukimarimo – naturally formed frost balls – at the South Pole Station during a sunrise in 2008.

what you would call a varied environment, it would be doing it a disservice to think of it as entirely homogenous. Deep crevasses can form where the ice sheet meets an obstacle, such as a nunatak or an ice shelf, although they are less common in comparatively featureless interior regions such as the Pole. However, as the early explorers discovered the hard way, the snow surface is also subject to other topographic features: it can be eroded by the wind into a series of peaks, troughs and ridges. These are termed, in the plural, 'sastrugi' (a term originally deriving from Russian). In areas of high katabatic winds they can be a couple of metres tall, although at the Pole they are much smaller. Moreover, while the Pole looks flat from the air, it sits on a slope – what Paul Siple, the scientific leader of the first group to winter there in 1957, called a 'very gentle hillside', so that one horizon is much closer than its opposite.[10] The changing response of this first group to their surrounds, as reported by Siple, is revealing:

> when the men first came to the Pole what most impressed each in turn was the 'nothingness' of this southernmost spot. There was no other place in the world where there was less to look at. The eye could not feast on a distant mountain, the ocean, birds, foliage – or even a crevasse. The nearest mountain peak lay 300 miles away and the

> ocean was 800 miles off. But as they began looking closer, they saw new things each time. There was beauty in the snow surface that was not apparent at the outset. The snow had different shapes and forms, from massive drifts to sastrugi-carved fields and on down to exquisite tiny crystals. Optical phenomena were all about us and some of them were awesome. We may have been people in solitary confinement, but the beauty of what lay around us was awe-inspiring.[11]

The optical phenomena to which Siple refers include the 'Southern Lights' or 'Aurora Australis', visible during the long polar night, as well as a host of other effects when the sun is in the sky, such as solar halos, 'parhelia' or 'sun dogs', solar pillars, and blue and green 'flashes'. All are visible elsewhere in the world but are more commonly seen and particularly spectacular in the polar regions. Best-known are the auroras, waving bands of

The Dome at Amundsen-Scott South Pole Station is seen above a field of sastrugi – ridges of snow formed by wind erosion – in late October 2003.

coloured lights in the night sky, most often green, but also red and violet. Robert F. Scott's journal entry, written at Cape Evans on midwinter's day in 1911, evokes the phenomenon with characteristic eloquence:

> The eastern sky was massed with swaying auroral light . . . fold on fold the arches and curtains of vibrating luminosity rose and spread across the sky, to slowly fade and yet again spring to glowing life . . . It is impossible to witness such a beautiful phenomenon without a sense of awe, and yet this sentiment is not inspired by its brilliancy but rather by its delicacy in light and colour, its transparency, and above all by its tremulous evanescence of form. There is no glittering splendour to dazzle the eye, as has been too often described; rather the appeal is to the imagination by the suggestion of something wholly spiritual, something instinct with a fluttering ethereal life, serenely confident yet restlessly mobile.[12]

Auroras are produced by the interaction between the Earth's magnetic field and the solar wind, a constant stream of charged particles issuing from the sun. These interactions can accelerate electrons down magnetic field lines and towards the Earth. Here they excite oxygen and nitrogen atoms in the atmosphere, which emit light at particular wavelengths when they relax towards a normal state – hence the colours of the display. Auroral activity is normally concentrated in an oval-shaped band surrounding the Geomagnetic Pole, although during periods of increased solar activity the band can shift, distort and expand so that auroral effects are visible further north in the southern hemisphere. A number of Antarctic stations, including South Pole, sit near to the zone (Australia's Mawson and Japan's Syowa, both coastal stations, are particularly well placed in this regard). Thus the sky, during the Pole's six-month night, is often lit up by waving curtains of light.

Another impressive phenomenon is the 'halos' – 'arcs or spots of light in the sky' – caused by the refraction and reflection of light through crystals suspended in the atmosphere.[13] They can

Sun dogs with halo at the base of Mount Vinson.

be produced by moonlight or artificial light – the 'ring around the moon' is a well-known example – but solar halos are the most spectacular. They can take a variety of forms – rings, arcs, 'mock suns', pillars – in different combinations, depending on factors such as the shape of the crystals, their orientation to the sun, and the sun's elevation. In lower, warmer latitudes, they tend to occur when the sun is high in the sky, because ice crystals are here confined to the upper atmosphere. They can be seen every few days in highly populated parts of the world, but tend not be noticed: although it is not unusual to look up at the moon, few people regularly look up at the sun. In very cold climates, ice crystals are suspended close to the Earth's surface, so these effects happen right before people's eyes.[14] The Pole, with its low, six-month sun and extremely cold temperatures, is an ideal place for viewing impressive and often quite rare halos.

Accounts of Antarctic exploration frequently contain descriptions of these effects. The meteorologist on Scott's second expedition, George Simpson, lectured to his companions about various atmospheric phenomena, which they in turn marvelled at on their travels:

> This morning it was calm and clear save for a light misty veil of ice crystals through which the moon shone with scarce

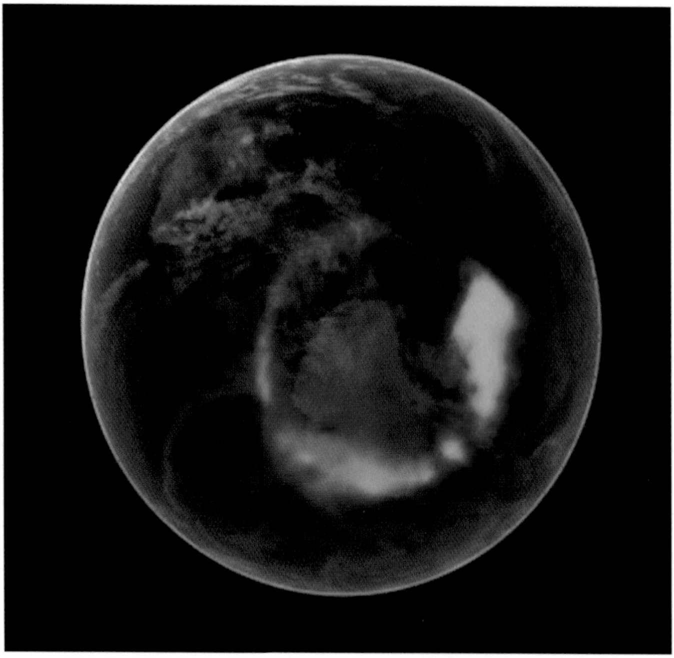

NASA satellite-generated view of the Aurora Australis in September 2005.

> clouded brilliancy, surrounded with bright cruciform halo and white paraselene. Mock moons with prismatic patches of colour appeared in the radiant ring, echoes of the main source of light. Wilson has a charming sketch of the phenomenon.[15]

The 'mock moons' (paraselenae) to which Scott refers are also known as 'moon dogs' – bright spots appearing on either side of the moon itself (or sometimes just on one side). The daytime equivalents – 'parhelia' or 'sun dogs' – are, along with the ring, the most commonly encountered halo. The spectacular sky shows best known to most humans – sunrise and sunset – each occur only once a year at the South Pole. However, the sun's disc takes more than a day to make its full transit below or above the horizon, and the whole process of sunrise and sunset is elongated, with twilight continuing for weeks. Particular optical effects, such as the 'green flash' – a burst of green light, normally a few seconds long, that occurs just as the top of the sun is disappearing below the horizon – can last intermittently for hours.[16]

For the aesthete and the atmospheric scientist, then, the South Pole has plenty of variation; but for the animal lover and the biologist, there is little on offer. Outside the station infrastructure, no life above the microbial level can exist at the South Pole. The only native creature to have ventured there is a south polar skua – a large Antarctic seabird. Scott reported seeing one on his fateful polar journey while camped at around 87 degrees south, 300 km (185 miles) from the Pole: 'an extraordinary visitor considering our distance from the sea'.[17] There are later reports of skuas occasionally visiting the interior of the plateau, including the

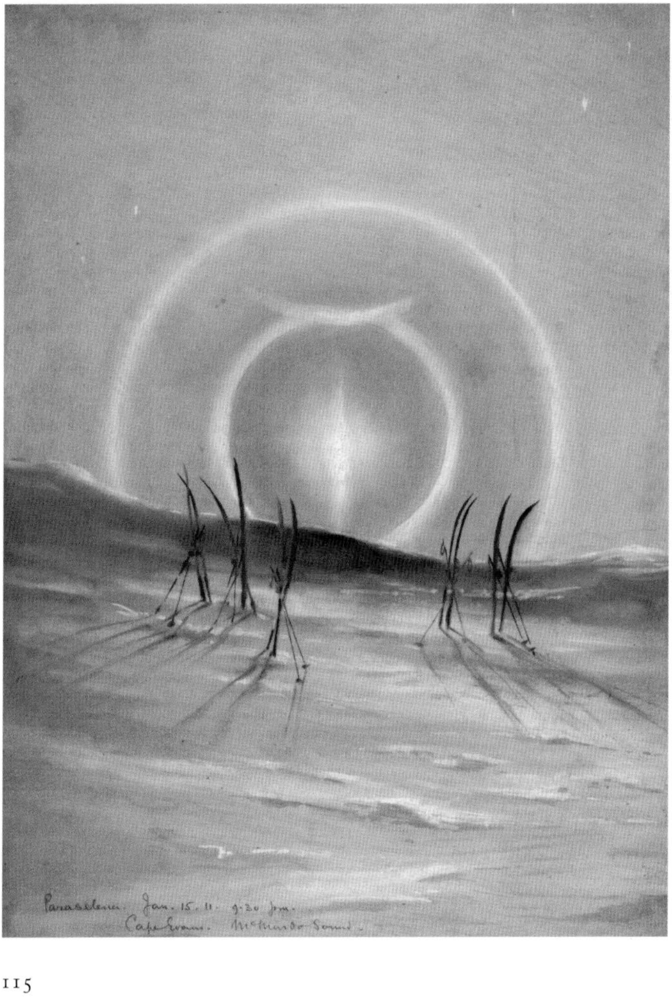

Edward Wilson's watercolour of a halo display, painted in mid-January 1911 at Cape Evans.

Sun dog at 89 degrees south.

Pole.[18] A snow petrel might also, at a stretch, make the distance – they have been recorded as far south as 85.5 degrees.[19]

Things are very different on the warmer coastal parts of the continent – a reminder that Antarctica is a heterogeneous place, not all of one piece. Life at its edges is far more evident, although most of the animals that can be found on land rely primarily on the marine ecosystem – the cold, rich waters around the continent – rather than the terrestrial environment.[20] Marine mammals that ply Antarctic waters and breed on its ice include Weddell, leopard, crabeater and Ross seals. They eat fish and krill (and penguins, in the case of the leopard seal), and in turn are menaced by orcas. Elephant seals breed on subantarctic islands but are summer visitors to the Antarctic continent, hauling out on beaches to moult. Several species of whale including humpbacks, fins, minkes and the largest of all living animals, blue whales, travel down to take advantage of the plentiful food supplies in the freezing water.

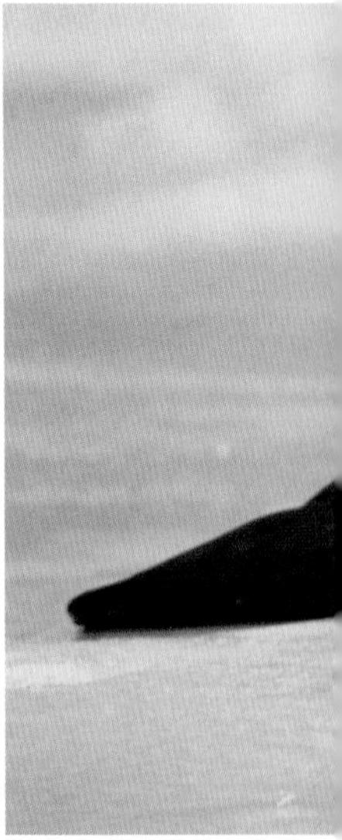

While penguins are automatically associated with the South Pole, this is an example of the term being used as shorthand for Antarctica. As aquatic birds, penguins inhabit the continent's coastal areas and fast ice, as well as the subantarctic islands and, indeed, various locations up to the equator. There are four species that live and breed on or very near the continent – chinstraps, gentoos, emperors and Adélies – although it is the last two of these that are considered 'true' Antarctic penguins, since they breed further south and are better adapted to the continent's environment. The closest that penguins come to the Pole itself is more than 1,370 km (850 miles) away, at the Adélie colony at Cape Royds on Ross Island. Many other bird species, such as skuas and petrels, can be found on and around the Antarctic coast. Ever since the publication of Coleridge's poem 'The Rime of the Ancient Mariner', Antarctica has been irrevocably associated with the albatross, but these birds mostly haunt higher latitudes of the southern ocean, and no species breed on the continent.

In the main, Antarctic terrestrial life consists of invertebrates, but even this is limited. Midges can be found in the comparatively mild conditions of the Antarctic Peninsula, but no insects exist in the rest of the continent, although mites, springtails and nematodes manage to survive in ice-free areas. Vegetation is largely confined to the coast; two flowering plants can be found on the Peninsula, but mosses, lichens and algae make up most of the plant life further south.[21] Lichen is the hardiest of Antarctic plants; it appears on and in exposed rock in the middle of the plateau, as close as 260 km (160 miles) to the Pole.[22]

A baby Weddell seal.

Inside the station, non-human life can survive but is forbidden: the 1991 'Madrid Protocol', part of the Antarctic Treaty System, stipulates the exclusion of all non-native organisms from the continent bar humans. Permits can be obtained only for specific approved uses, such as domestic plants for food. Amundsen-Scott base includes a hydroponic greenhouse that doubles as a therapeutic space of escape for its human occupants. Inhabitants of the Pole clearly feel the lack of the non-human life that coastal stations enjoy: 'Plastic flowers are planted in the snow outside some buildings. On a desk a magnetic fish lurches in its fishbowl, and in the Galley a plastic potted smiling flower dances to loud noises.'[23] Dogs, of course, have been at the Pole as long as humans. One of the first human acts there was the slaughtering of one: the men of the Norwegian Antarctic Expedition regularly killed their failing dogs as food for the remaining animals as well as themselves, and they made no exception at their South Pole camp. Helmar Hanssen reluctantly dispatched with a blow to the head his 'best friend' Helge, who was 'portioned out on the spot'.[24] Almost half a century later, dogs were back: the crew that built the first station at the Pole included huskies, who 'led a neglected life'.[25] This early inclusion of huskies notwithstanding, the U.S. does not have an extensive history of using working sledge dogs, unlike some other national programmes. Huskies as station pets, however, were not unusual at the Pole until the mid-1970s, when a no-pet policy was enforced at U.S. stations; after that, dogs occasionally arrived with adventurers making polar traverses.[26] Laboratory animals were another distraction (and are still allowed under permit): hamsters were introduced at the Pole in 1960 for the purpose of metabolic studies, and twin baby hamsters were born there in 1961.

Emperor penguin.

Emperor penguins appear mildly interested in a Twin-Otter aircraft that has landed tourists on sea ice at the continent's coast.

A surprising range of introduced animals have made the voyage to the edge of continent, brought accidentally in the holds of ships, or deliberately as food, working animals or pets. They include cats, rats, mice, horses, donkeys, cows, sheep, goats, pigs, hedgehogs and a bat. Dogs are the only introduced animals that have survived unaided for a substantial length of time in the Antarctic environment. The most famous example occurred when the Japanese coastal base Syowa had to be evacuated quickly in early 1958, and fifteen Karafuto dogs were reluctantly abandoned. When the next wintering team arrived a year later, two dogs had survived. They went on to become national celebrities. Despite the strictures of the Madrid Protocol, there are still occasional reports of dogs or cats loose on the continent.[27]

In the deep past, of course, native flora and fauna would have been spread across the whole Antarctic continent. Antarctica has not always stood in proud isolation at the Pole. Many hundreds of millions of years ago, East Antarctica may well have been joined to the western coast of North America, as part of the northern hemisphere supercontinent Rodinia. Around 500

The South Pole Food Growth Chamber: this hydroponic, artificially lit greenhouse provides fresh food for the expeditioners.

million years ago it formed a central part of Gondwana, joined to Africa, India, South America and Australia. Northwest Africa lay over the Geographic Pole, while Antarctica was in low southern latitudes. Originally near the equator, Gondwana shifted and broke apart over the next few hundred million years. As the continent moved through different latitudes, it was 'colonised by an evolving flora and fauna': big rivers, lakes and seas where fish swam; swamps filled with vegetation; trees such as conifers, gingkos and ferns; large reptiles, dinosaurs and amphibians.[28] Palaeontologists can piece together this history from fossils found in the nunataks jutting out of the ice: Scott's doomed party famously spent hours 'geologising' on their return from the Pole, dragging back to their last camp 13.6 kg (30 lb) of rocks, including fossil specimens of *Glossopteris* – an ancient fern – confirming the continent's early links to India and Australia. By 32 million years ago Antarctica had arrived at its polar location and had broken off from Australia, New Zealand and South America. The circumpolar current began to flow, the continent grew cooler and the plants changed. Beeches, mosses and conifers grew within a few hundred miles of the Pole and there is evidence of tundra and shrubs in the continent's interior until around

14 million years ago.[29] While the continents will keep shifting into the far future, Antarctica is likely to stay over the South Pole, rotating anticlockwise, for the next 50 million years.[30]

Ancient life means coal, now visible as 'thick . . . seams stretching along the length of the Transantarctic Mountains' – as well as oil and gas.[31] The continent's potential mineral resources were certainly on the mind of early explorers such as the geologist Mawson. Science fiction writers of the mid-twentieth century got excited about the possibilities, writing stories with titles such as 'South Polar Beryllium, Limited'.[32] Over the years, a number of different minerals have indeed been found in the region, including lead, zinc, copper, silver, gold, tin, nickel, cobalt, manganese, chromium, titanium and uranium.[33] The discovery in the Prince Charles Mountains of the mineral kimberlite, in which diamond is sometimes present, generated media interest. However, the Antarctic presents numerous obstacles to miners: the lack of exposed areas, the thickness of the ice, the difficulties negotiating sea ice and icebergs, the isolation and environmental extremes. Places high on the ice sheet away from mountains, such as the South Pole, are particularly unlikely sites for mineral exploitation. Moreover, with the exception of iron and coal, there is no direct evidence that any minerals are present in the continent in large enough quantities even to warrant the term 'deposits'.[34] Some estimates of oil and gas quantities based on Antarctica's geology, however, suggest commercial potential, and it remains possible that parts of the region, including the continental shelves, might be viable for future exploitation if resources elsewhere are scarce enough, prices high enough and technology sufficiently developed.

The prospect of mining in and around Antarctica really came to public attention in the 1970s, after the international oil crisis. In the late 1980s the Convention on the Regulation of Antarctic Mineral Resource Activities (CRAMRA) was adopted as part of the Antarctic Treaty System as a precautionary attempt to put rules in place in case the region did become accessible to commercial mining. However, this action was opposed from various angles. Environmental groups such as Greenpeace protested against the potential despoliation of the wilderness, asking

overleaf: This satellite image of the Larsen B Ice Shelf from early 2000 shows pools of meltwater and icebergs splintering off. The shelf collapsed in 2002.

instead for World Park status. Developing nations – particularly Malaysia – voiced concerns that the region would be divided up by richer nations, and suggested that Antarctica be managed instead by the United Nations.[35] This controversy meant that Australia and France refused to sign the Convention; other nations soon joined them. The result was the Protocol on Environmental Protection to the Antarctic Treaty or 'Madrid Protocol', mentioned earlier. Signed in 1991 and entering into force in 1998, the Protocol included, among other things, an indefinite ban on mining (the Protocol can be reviewed in 2048).

Another form of 'mining' has been happening in Antarctica for decades. 'Bioprospecting' – searching for naturally occurring biological substances that can be used for health or other benefits – has obvious potential in Antarctica, where the extreme environment produces organisms with unusual capabilities. A prominent example is the antifreeze glycoproteins produced by the group of fish called notothenioids (such as the Antarctic toothfish). First discovered in the late 1960s, these biological agents prevent the fishes' body fluids forming ice crystals in sub-zero temperatures. They could have a range of applications, from preserving tissues more effectively during transplant surgery to prolonging the shelf-life of frozen food. It is not just the continent's rich surrounding waters at stake here, however; the ice itself and subglacial lakes can also be home to 'extremophiles', and present potentially useful – and lucrative – resources for bioprospectors. However, the activity, enabled by scientists supported by national programmes in a continent that is still unowned, raises many legal, ethical, commercial and environmental issues, which are currently being debated by Antarctic Treaty nations.

A far more high-profile threat to Antarctica's current environment is global warming. The continent is playing a crucial part in climate change science and political debate, in several senses: as a tool for understanding climate variation; as a region that may be severely affected by warming temperatures; and as the possible source of disastrous impact on the rest of the globe, should its ice sheets become unstable. The ice sheets store

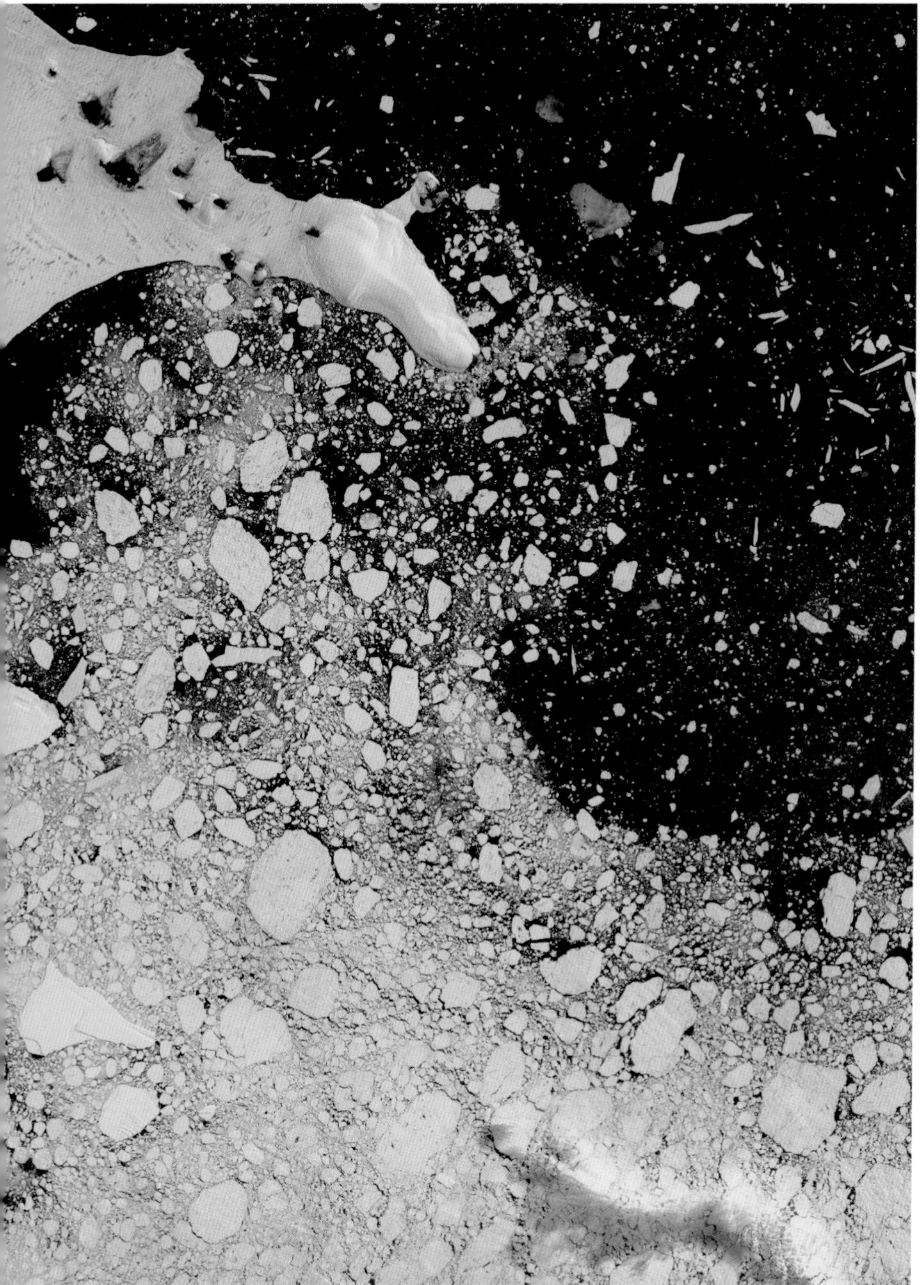

millions of years' worth of climate data that, retrieved in the form of ice cores, demonstrates the connection between increased atmospheric carbon dioxide and temperature, and provides a background of natural variation against which current changes can be compared.[36]

The impact of anthropogenic climate change on the region is more complex: while East Antarctica is thus far little affected, the waters around the continent and West Antarctica – particularly the Antarctic Peninsula – are warming. Spectacularly, several large ice shelves have broken off the Peninsula. In 2002 the enormous Larsen B shelf, having stayed stable since the last ice age, collapsed – an event scientists believe is related to anthropogenic changes to atmospheric circulation.[37] The West Antarctic ice sheet is increasingly losing mass due largely to the interaction between the warmer ocean and its marine glaciers.[38] The potential impact of a melting Antarctica is catastrophic. The continent contains ten times more ice than the rest of the Earth put together: an increase in temperature of several degrees could cause the collapse of the whole West Antarctic ice sheet, producing a sea level rise of about 1.5 m (5 ft).[39] If the much larger East Antarctica sheet were eventually also to collapse, the net rise would be around 58 m (190 ft). It is the grounded ice that would produce this rise, as opposed to ice that already displaces water, such as floating ice and ice below sea level.[40]

Where does this leave the Geographic South Pole? Neither high nor dry, if all the Antarctic ice were to melt. This worst case scenario is not likely in the foreseeable future, but climate models show that future temperature changes will be amplified on the Antarctic plateau, about 20 per cent higher than average. The South Pole would be several degrees warmer – a scenario that has occurred before in interglacial periods, with a corresponding sea-level rise.[41] The poles – defined as the points where the planet's axis meets its surface – will shift as a result of this melting: redistribution of water can change the location of the planet's rotational axis. Research has shown that the North Pole, drifting on average southwards along the 70 degrees west meridian over the last century or so, has recently made a lurch to the east, most likely due to increased rates of melting ice.[42] The South Pole, it stands to reason, must have made its own shift. Only a century ago, humans had barely reached the poles; now, it seems, we have inadvertently managed to move them.

7 Looking Up and Looking Down

The South Pole's unusual combination of physical features gives it peculiar advantages as a site for scientific investigation. However, the science that takes place *at* the South Pole is not necessarily *about* the place itself. There is no wildlife to observe there, no trees or flowers to study, no exposed rock to examine. Instead, the Pole is an excellent place to look *from*, whether this is up into space or down into the ice – or into the core of the Earth. Research that seems very local can have global – even cosmic – significance.

Not just the Pole but the whole polar plateau offers itself as a site for research. The plateau's physical extremes – its status as the highest, driest, coldest, most isolated and, for some months of the year, darkest region on Earth – bring unique scientific advantages. There are, admittedly, specific benefits for some experiments in being on the Earth's rotation axis (the Pole itself). For much scientific work, however, there are many places on the plateau, including other stations, that are as good as or better than 90 degrees south, judged purely on environmental conditions. The Pole's advantage – ironically, for the 'last' place on Earth – is its comparative accessibility and pre-existing infrastructure. Heavy equipment can be flown in and out by U.S. military aircraft or hauled across the ice on motorized vehicles along a pre-smoothed 'road'. Scientific and support personnel in the hundreds can be accommodated in the station and nearby 'summer camp'.

A wide variety of scientific experiments take place at the South Pole. Its clean air, which is free from most of the usual

An image of Earth in September 2005 with the entire Antarctic region visible.

local pollutants, is used to determine wide-scale changes to atmospheric composition; levels of carbon dioxide and ozone have been continually monitored for around 50 years. In its long winter darkness, auroras are studied for what they can tell us about space weather (the environmental conditions of the region of space near Earth). NASA uses the interior of Antarctica as an analogue for the terrain and temperatures of Earth's neighbouring planet Mars. Even scientists themselves become subjects of study by psychologists interested in the dynamics of isolated groups. However, the South Polar science that attracts most attention – and costs the most money – involves examining data found in the sky above or the ice below.

Antarctica provides the world's best conditions for astronomical research. While some forms of astrophysics can be conducted from coastal bases such as McMurdo and Mawson stations, it is the plateau that offers astronomers 'the best seeing conditions, the darkest skies and the most transparent atmosphere'.[1] The plateau's primary attraction for astronomers (who use numerous techniques, including optical, radio and infrared telescopes) is its

Unoccupied, snow-covered Jamesway huts wait for the summer station population to arrive.

NASA's robot explorer 'Tumbleweed', a prototype of a device that could be used to look for water on the Martian icescape, was released at the Pole in 2004, making a 70-km (43-mile) journey over the plateau.

high, cold, dry and isolated location. For telescopes looking at the microwave and infrared radiation arriving from deep space, the dry air is paramount. Water vapour absorbs and re-emits the radiation, interfering with the data. Both the height of the plateau and the cold temperature reduce water vapour significantly. In addition, the dryer the atmosphere, the more uniform it is; the 'noise' of local fluctuations is reduced.[2] The isolation means that anthropogenic disturbances such as aerosols, aircraft contrails and light pollution are minimized.

The Pole itself (as opposed to the plateau more generally) has both pros and cons as an astronomical site. The six months of darkness mean that problematic diurnal temperature changes are absent; moreover, if your telescope is at the Earth's axis of rotation, it has continuous access to the same area of sky.[3] Visible objects stay at the same elevation, rather than rising and setting, meaning that the amount of atmosphere you look through stays constant, resulting in more stable observations. However, located on the slope rather than the centre of the plateau, the Pole is lower than some other possible plateau sites, slightly windier (creating less stable air conditions near the surface), cloudier and more subject to interference from auroral activity.[4] Dome A is

The South Pole Telescope at twilight, 2012.

probably the best of the occupied inland sites for astronomical projects, with Dome F also very favourable, and the presently uninhabited Ridge A (running southwest from Dome A) the best site of all.[5] However, while several plateau stations do include astronomical research – such as the PLATeau Observatory (PLATO) at Dome A, robotically controlled to run year-round – the station facilities and the ability to fly large amounts of equipment in mean that the primary site of Antarctic astronomy and astrophysics has been the South Pole.[6]

Astronomical research at the South Pole began in 1979 with observations of the sun over a long continuous period, and really took off in the early 1990s with the construction of the Martin A. Pomerantz Observatory (MAPO), named after the scientist who had led many of the early experiments.[7] Like other instruments used by astronomers and astrophysicists, this observatory sits in the 'Dark Sector', located across the compact-snow skiway from the station, where light and radio pollution are kept to a minimum. While a range of projects are under way at any one time, the investigation of the Cosmic Microwave Background

Radiation (CMBR) has been particularly prominent. CMBR is the background 'glow' left over from the explosion that began the universe, the 'Big Bang'; it is strongest in the microwave section of the electromagnetic spectrum. While this radiation is largely uniform, small variations provide information about the early universe and hence about its current structure. Observations of stellar explosions have shown that the universe is expanding at an accelerating rate, despite the opposing force of gravity, suggesting the existence of another mysterious entity, dubbed 'Dark Energy'. This phenomenon, among others, is investigated using the South Pole Telescope (SPT), a 10-m (33-ft) radio telescope that sits white and strangely beautiful against the horizon. Built at a cost of more than $19 million, the SPT began collecting data in 2007. A neighbouring telescope, BICEP2, has made major contributions to understanding the universe's beginning: in 2014 it identified the influence on the CMBR of gravitational waves that occurred in an unimaginably small instant following the Big Bang. This in turn confirmed the theory that the very early universe experienced a period of 'inflation', or exponentially accelerating expansion. This data could also shed light on the fundamental issue of how quantum physics and relativity are connected.[8] The South Pole, the symbolic 'last place', may

A flagline in the 'Dark Sector' helps people to find their way during the long Antarctic night. The South Pole Telescope can just be seen on the horizon.

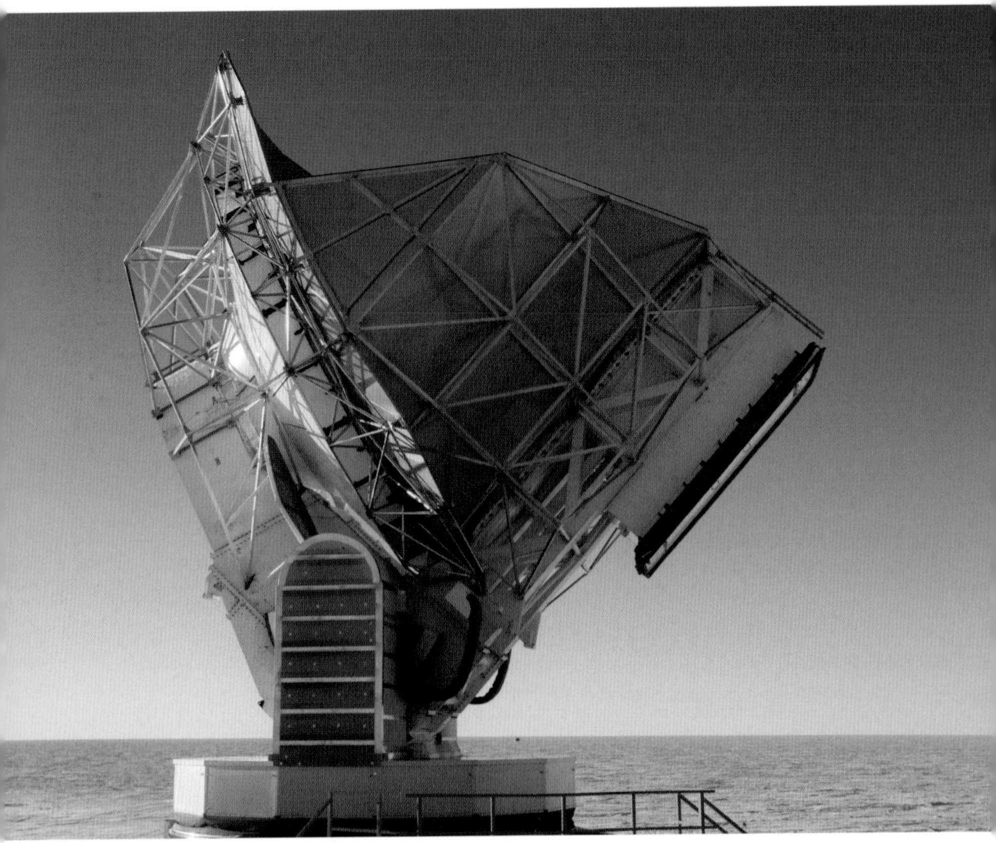

A closer shot of the South Pole Telescope (SPT), with some new additions, in 2013.

have provided an important step in the search for a 'Theory of Everything'.

Less visible than the SPT but equally high-profile is the experiment buried within the ice: the IceCube Neutrino Observatory. Costing USD$279 million, IceCube began operating in 2010. Where the SPT takes advantage of the height of the plateau to look up at the stars, IceCube exploits the depth of the ice, using it as a giant telescope to watch for elusive particles. These are tiny, almost massless neutrinos, which travel very close to the speed of light. Neutrinos are another key to understanding the structure and evolution of the universe. If a neutrino collides with other particles, this event can be detected from the light it produces. However, because the particles are so small and uncharged, these interactions are very rare: if the detecting area were human-sized, it would take around 100 years for an event to occur – 100,000 years in the energy range that IceCube can detect. The larger the detector, the more often you will see an interaction; IceCube uses a cubic kilometre of ice. More than 5,000 detectors are buried between 1,450 and 2,450 m (4,760 and 8,040 ft) below the surface of the plateau, attached to cables placed in 86 holes made using hot-water drills. The darkness and clearness of the ice is ideal for detection: IceCube observes about 275 neutrinos every day. And although the ice moves 10 metres per year, it moves in one piece, so the experiment remains intact.[9] As with the SPT, the immense size of the project, along with the enigmatic nature of the particles it is designed to observe, creates a cachet that is reinforced by its glamorously remote South Polar location.

Another group of scientists who look down from the South Pole are seismologists. The South Pole is an excellent place to study earthquakes, but not because Antarctica is particularly prone to this phenomenon. On the contrary, it suffers the least number of tremors of any continent. Again, this is a case of science using the South Pole to look elsewhere: its position at the spin axis means that the Earth's rotational forces do not affect measurements as they do in other places, so seismic events elsewhere in the planet can be observed with an unusual clarity. The North Pole also has this advantage, but there is no Arctic continent to which recording equipment might be secured.[10]

The most recent seismological station – one of a global cooperative network – is housed in the South Pole Remote Earth Science Observatory (SPRESO), located in the Quiet Sector, 8 km (5 miles) away from the main station building, where vibrations and noise produced by equipment and vehicles are kept to a minimum. To achieve even less interference, seismometers have been buried 300 m (1,000 ft) down into the ice. As a result, they can record 'the quietest vibrations on Earth, up to 4 times quieter than ever before observed'.[11] This means that SPRESO can detect seismic activity that has propagated through the Earth from distant regions of the globe, gathering data about the planet's internal structure. As the science writer Gabrielle Walker explains, the observatory 'could act as a sort of inward telescope, constructing an image of the Earth's mantle of rock, its liquid outer core made of almost pure iron, and the hot hard solid sphere of iron that lies at the centre of the Earth'.[12] Studies of seismic activities were a crucial part of the original station's programme in the late 1950s, and now form the longest-running of any scientific data set at the Pole. They provide evidence that the Earth's solid core spins more quickly than the rest of the planet.[13] And SPRESO can also detect anthropogenic disturbances to the planet: it acts as a monitoring station for the Comprehensive Nuclear-Test-Ban Treaty. The very lack of activity – lack of spin, lack of noise – means that it is a unique place from which to listen to the hustle and bustle of the rest of the globe.

Scientists seem to be drilling enough holes at the Pole at present to satisfy even John Cleves Symmes Jr. Where the IceCube physicists bury their neutrino detectors deep in the ice to create a giant telescope, and the seismologists of SPRESO lodge their detectors hundreds of metres down to escape extraneous noise, glaciologists drill down to examine the ice itself – or rather, the atmospheric traces it contains. Retrieving and analysing ice cores is one of the most urgent and important scientific activities in Antarctica. An ice core is a continuous vertical sample drilled from an ice sheet or glacier, stored in cylindrical sections about a couple of metres long. These are, in a sense, solidified representations of time. Analysis of materials in the ice, including dust, volcanic ash and trapped gas, provides information about the Earth's environment over past periods, such as temperature and levels of carbon dioxide – something of vital importance to understanding and contextualizing current changes in climate.

In any one place, if there has not been significant faulting or folding, the deeper the ice from which the core is retrieved, the longer ago it was deposited. However, the varied rate of snow accumulation in the Antarctic interior means that the equation between depth and time changes from place to place. High up on the plateau, the snow accumulation is very low, with the result that the kilometres of ice offer a very long record. Vostok Station is well situated for examining long-term climate variation through ice cores. A 150,000-year, 2-kilometre core recovered in the late 1980s, followed by a 420,000-year, 3.3-kilometre core in 1996, provided important data showing the link between temperature and carbon dioxide in the atmosphere.[14] Along with other ice cores, such as the 800,000-year, 2.8-kilometre sample recovered at Dome C, they offer a record of natural variation against which current changes can be compared, establishing evidence for anthropogenic climate change.

At the South Pole, snow accumulation is significantly faster than at Vostok, and the ice is correspondingly younger; records are thus shorter but finer in their detail.[15] The South Pole Ice Core project (with the appealing acronym SPICE) aims to retrieve a 1,500 metre ice-core, representing about 40,000 years – not much in terms of time compared to the core recovered at Dome C. Its resolution, however, is expected to be the highest of any East Antarctic core.[16] The movement of the ice is another factor: the South Pole core 'should offer relatively well-ordered stratigraphy, meaning the layers are well defined and the youngest layers are on top and the oldest layers are on the bottom, with no evidence of folding or faulting in between'. As with much South Polar science, however, the 'logistical support' already available at the station is a strong factor in the location of the experiment.[17]

Science has always been the *raison d'être* for human settlement at the South Pole – officially, at least. The first South Pole station began as a part of a planet-wide coordinated scientific effort, the 1957–8 International Geophysical Year. Over half a century and two new stations later, some activities (such as air

Researcher working with an ice core drill.

sampling) have remained essentially the same, while others (such as cosmology) have expanded in ways that could never have been anticipated. The South Pole is the symbolic centre of the land variously called a 'continent for science' or 'giant natural laboratory'. Yet all Antarctic scientists know that the science they produce, no matter how impressive, is a means as well as an end – a legitimate way of maintaining national presence in a continent where resources are still, in a sense, up for grabs. To understand how science became the 'currency of credibility' for any nation wanting a say about Antarctica, you need to understand South Polar politics.[18]

8 South Polar Politics

Near the beginning of Ariel Dorfman's novel *The Nanny and the Iceberg* (1999), the protagonist, Gabriel McKenzie – a young boy living in New York in the early 1980s – sneaks out of a Chilean resistance meeting to which he has been dragged by his expatriate mother. Rejecting her politics, he walks along the city streets and becomes enthralled by images playing on the television sets in a shop window:

> I allowed myself to dally there for an hour watching the same images repeated on twenty-five fractured screens, those mountains of ice floating on a sea that was black with waves, those caverns of snow and fog that I saw for the first time that evening, that soundless special on Antarctica that I watched, entranced, from the other side of the window. At that moment, of course, I had no idea that the Chile I had just repudiated had any connection whatsoever with that extraordinary forbidden world I was discovering and devouring with my eyes. It is only now that I see how ironic and fateful it is that on the very night I declared my unilateral independence from my country I was waylaid by images of a silent crystal continent that was part of the territory of that country . . .[1]

Like Gabriel, many people assume that the Antarctic represents a complete escape from politics – a realm of pure natural spectacle, trammelled only by a small band of altruistic scientists. In reality it is a politically complex and contested region, subject to ongoing international negotiation. The Antarctic Peninsula – the site of overlapping and unresolved national claims by Chile, Argentina and Britain – is the subject of the most intense rivalry. Gabriel's assertion that Antarctica is 'part of the territory' of his country is itself a disputable political statement. As the narrative continues, he becomes involved in a nationalistic endeavour (based on an actual historical event) to drag an Antarctic iceberg northwards in order to display it in the Chilean Pavilion at the 1992 Universal Exposition in Spain.

While the Peninsula may be the subject of more obvious dispute than any other part of Antarctica, the Geographic South Pole is arguably the most politically potent site because of its symbolic value as the 'heart' of the continent. This certainly seems to have been the view of the U.S. government and its allies when plans were made to build a research station there during the International Geophysical Year (IGY) of 1957–8. The station's first scientific leader Paul Siple's account of U.S. activities in the 1940s and '50s frankly identifies 'potential sovereignty' as a significant motivation. Although initially reluctant for logistical reasons to build an IGY station at the Pole, the U.S. took on the task when, at a meeting in 1955, 'the Russians dropped a bombshell' – their own plans to put a station there. The interest of Antarctic hero Richard Byrd, one of the forces behind the station's construction, 'went far beyond the IGY', Siple recalled. 'He wanted it said, as did I, that the United States had done the impossible. A fierce national pride burned within him.' However, when Siple, having lived at the station for a year, was asked whom it belonged to, his reply reflected the political complexity of the situation: 'The U.S. taxpayers paid for the buildings, of course . . . But six countries' claims intersect that ring of barrels out there on the drop zone.'[2]

This strange situation was the result of claim-making in the Antarctic that, while incorporating events stretching back hundreds of years, centred on national exploratory and legal activities during the first half of the twentieth century. Many of the early explorers made gestures towards national possession of parts of the continent by flag-planting, place-naming and proclamation

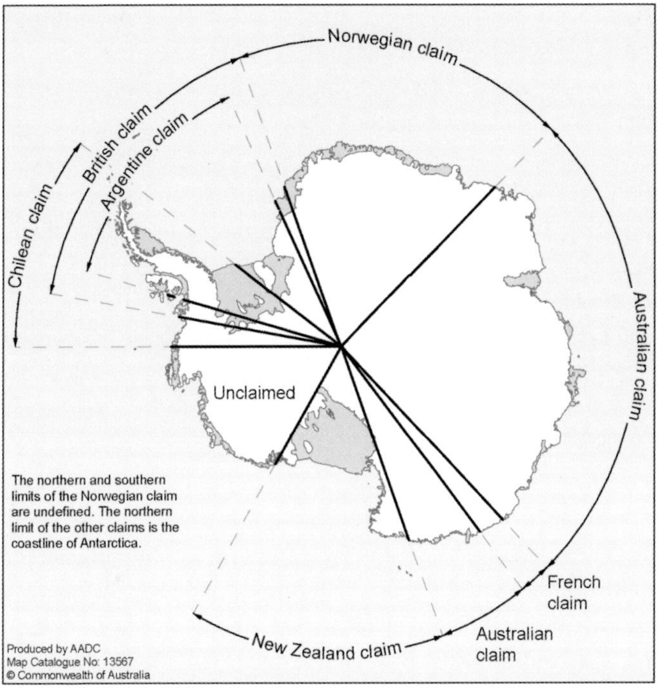

Map showing territorial claims.

ceremonies. Amundsen, for example, considered the 'greatest and most solemn act' of his polar journey to be the flying of the Norwegian flag at his destination: 'Thus we plant thee, beloved flag, at the South Pole, and give to the plain on which it lies the name of King Haakon VII's Plateau.' Scott certainly promoted his second expedition in nationalistic as well as scientific terms: 'it appeals to our national pride and the maintenance of great traditions, and its quest becomes an outward visible sign that we are still a nation able and willing to undertake difficult enterprises, still capable of standing in the van of the army of progress'.[3] Nobu Shirase's quest for the South Pole 'caught the popular imagination of a people . . . determined to show that their nation was ready and willing to take its place on the stage of world affairs'.[4] His expedition marked their furthest south by raising a Japanese flag on a 2-metre-high bamboo pole and naming the surrounding snow plain 'Yamato', once used as a name for Japan. The official expedition narrative includes a stirring address to the snow plain itself: 'Thousands, nay, tens of thousands of years from now, indeed for as long as this Earth shall last may you prosper as the territory of Japan.'[5] Elsewhere in the continent a variety of other expressions of nationalism took place: Byrd, for example, dropped a U.S. flag over the Pole in his 1929 overflight, and other nations such as Australia and Germany undertook similar aerial flag-dropping exercises. These acts did not themselves translate into legal possession, although they often formed part of the basis for claims.

The first nation officially to declare sovereignty over part of Antarctica was Great Britain, which in 1908 claimed, as part of its Falkland Islands Dependency, the region between 20 and 80 degrees west – roughly below South America.[6] In 1917 it extended the southern boundary down to the Pole, thus claiming a pie-shaped wedge or 'sector' of the continent. By the end of the First World War, Britain was intent on eventually gaining control of the entire continent. During the following two decades the British Empire laid claim to two other sectors, one extending out from the Ross Sea, placed under the administration of New Zealand, and the Australian Antarctic Territory (AAT) in East Antarctica, which covered 42 per cent of the continent. Each extended to the Pole, following the 'sector principle'. A crucial part of the legal basis for these claims was the exploratory activities of the previous centuries, including the expeditions led by Cook and Ross, shored up by subsequent activity in the twentieth century.

Other nations did not simply stand by and watch as Britain advanced its territorial interests. Early on France had made clear to Britain its interest in a small wedge of East Antarctica, Terre Adélie ('Adélie Land'), on the basis of Dumont d'Urville's mid-nineteenth-century expedition, but did not define its limits until 1933. The sector sat amid the large area Britain had recently placed under Australia's authority. However, given its own similar legal arguments, Britain had little option but to recognize France's claim, which it officially did in 1938 after some negotiation between the two countries over which longitude lines should mark the boundaries.[7]

Norway, unsurprisingly, was concerned about Britain's claims, which encompassed parts of the continent discovered by its own explorers. It was only in 1939, however, to pre-empt a possible claim by Germany (the Third German Antarctic Expedition was then on its way south), that Norway declared sovereignty over Dronning Maud Land, between 20 degrees west and 45 degrees east – a sixth of the continent. This claim had little to do with the achievements of its most famous Antarctic hero.[8] The Norwegian government did not pursue its potential territorial interests in the area immediately around the Pole – the region Amundsen had named for Haakon VII. Indeed, Norway's is ironically the only Antarctic territorial claim that does *not* stretch to the Pole – its southern and northern boundaries are unspecified. Norway's decision hinged on its Arctic interests: because these would be endangered by a sector approach, Norway chose not to endorse this model in the south.

This eagerness of European nations to claim a large slab of frozen wilderness at the bottom of the world is explained partly by the rise of whaling activities in the area. Antarctic whaling had been developing on a significant scale since early in the twentieth century, first from stations on subantarctic islands such as South Georgia, then through the use of floating factory ships further south. Whale oil had a variety of uses, including soap and detergent, lubrication of machinery and margarine, which also

Norwegian postcard (1912) featuring artist Andreas Bloch's impression of Amundsen's team planting the national flag at the South Pole.

produced, as a by-product, glycerine, one of the ingredients of the explosive nitroglycerin. In the interwar period nations were eager to have access to this material, and with the Antarctic by far the most productive whaling ground at the time, this fed into territorial interests. Norway's claim to Dronning Maud Land was based largely on the whaling expeditions to the region led by Lars Christensen over the previous decades.[9] Nazi Germany's decision to launch an expedition to the same region was closely tied to its desire to secure its whaling industry.[10]

Up to this point, all claims had been made by European nations, resting largely on relatively recent exploration and activity in the region. In the 1940s Chile and Argentina entered the fray, basing their claims on a different set of associations. Both pointed to a late fifteenth-century Papal Bull and subsequent treaty that had divided any newly discovered lands along a vaguely specified meridian running through the Atlantic Ocean and South America, giving Spain the area to the west and Portugal that to the east. Making its first official claim in 1940, to a sector to its south overlapping territory claimed by Britain, Chile argued that the treaty encompassed land down to the South Pole, which it had inherited from Spain. Another argument was its geographic proximity to Antarctica. During the years that followed Argentina also made a claim, which had a similar basis, but included geological associations and long-standing continuing occupation: Argentina had manned a meteorological station on an island in the South Orkneys since 1904, the oldest of any Antarctic base. The Argentinian claim overlapped with both Chile's and Britain's, the latter intersection adding to the existing dispute over the Falkland/Malvinas islands.

There were now six claims meeting at the South Pole (the seventh claim, Norway's, being unspecified in its southerly extent). Only one sector – about one-fifth of the continent – was left unclaimed (and still is). While the European nations, Australia and New Zealand acknowledged each other's claims, they did not recognize those of the South American nations. In terms of international law, all the claims were weak. Papal Bulls issued half a millennium ago and geological arguments did not count for much in a modern legal context. Discovery and exploration were also insufficient unless they were solidified by permanent occupation of the region. This was, of course, challenging in the Antarctic. Britain argued for a watered-down version of occupation suited to the polar situation, based on 'administration' – the issuing of whaling licences, for example.

Meanwhile, Byrd's expeditions and flights had been colonizing the region around the Ross Sea literally and symbolically, with a series of bases called 'Little America', but no U.S. claim had been made. Siple, who had first travelled with Byrd as a Boy Scout, reflects in *90° South* on the oddity of the situation as he saw it: 'the United States, whose Antarctic explorations had uncovered more of the continent than the sum total of all claimants, had not raised its voice to demand a single foot of Antarctica'.[11] In 1924 the United States had adopted the 'Hughes Doctrine', which insisted upon occupation as a basis for territorial claims. Accordingly, it recognized no other Antarctic claims, but reserved the right to make its own.[12] In the next couple of decades it strengthened this right considerably, and appeared poised to make a claim on occasion, but none was forthcoming. There was a variety of reasons for this, not least that making a claim would mean recognizing others' and thus foreclosing possibilities: 'A claim could . . . diminish American freedom to move and establish bases anywhere on the continent.'[13] In 1948 the U.S. suggested the possibility of joining the seven claimants to form a 'condominium' in which sovereignty was shared. This had the advantage, for the U.S., of pre-empting possible Soviet advances. For the existing claimants, however, this would mean surrendering their national territorial rights in favour of joint sovereignty; the suggestion was rejected.

Given the unresolved and, in the case of some claimants, tense nature of this situation, it is no surprise that the U.S., if Siple's account of the lead-up to the International Geophysical Year is accurate, volunteered to build a base on the South Pole largely to stop the Soviets from doing so. The Geographic Pole, however, did not have a monopoly on symbolic power – there was a range of other poles to choose from. France decided to build a station close to the Magnetic South Pole, which at that point lay in Adélie Land, about 320 km (200 miles) from the coast. The Soviet Union located a base (Vostok) on the Geomagnetic Pole, a point even more logistically challenging than the South Pole. While the location was 'expected to be favourable for studying the ionosphere and the effects of magnetic storms', 'image and prestige' were important motivations for its selection.[14] To underline the point, the Soviets established another station – albeit a short-lived one – on the Pole of Inaccessibility, which seems to have had few advantages apart from the challenge it posed. 'Both superpowers', writes the political geographer Klaus Dodds, 'were making a powerful political and symbolic point – claimants

A signpost at Vostok Station gives distances to Moscow and other distant cities. The station was originally built on the Geomagnetic South Pole.

The Ceremonial Pole is framed by a semicircle of flags representing the twelve nations that were original signatories to the Antarctic Treaty.

had no special rights in the context of international scientific investigation.'[15] While there were scientific reasons put forward for all these 'pole positions', there were obviously politically strategic motivations as well, given that both nations, while making no claims of their own, reserved the right to a future claim over any or all of the continent.

While the IGY had seen an effective 'moratorium on claims', claimant nations were nonetheless nervous about possible encroachment on their 'territories' – a situation that intensified as the event came to a close. The scientific success of the IGY, combined with the complex political motivations of the twelve nations involved (in addition to the seven claimants, the U.S., USSR, Japan, Belgium and South Africa), led to the drawing up in late 1959 of the 'Antarctic Treaty'. This document, applicable to the region south of 60 degrees south, declares that Antarctica will be used 'exclusively for peaceful purposes' (military activities and nuclear weapons are banned) and that 'freedom of scientific investigation' should prevail. While sovereign claims cannot be strengthened or weakened while the treaty is in force, they continue to stand: 'all the claimant states continued to believe that their territorial claims were intact and fundamentally unchanged. Stamps continued to

Norwegian and Australian commemorative stamps.

be issued, textbooks authored, and maps drawn' proclaiming the various territories.[16] The South American nations populated stations with families and children; the first person born in Antarctica was an Argentinian boy in 1978. However, these claims, recognized only by certain other claimants, mean very little in practice: under the terms of the Treaty, other nations can undertake scientific research and build stations on the claimed territory. Moreover, although the Treaty has no expiration date, it does not prevent any state from making a new claim if it collapses at some time in the future.

Today, more than 50 years later, the Antarctic Treaty is still in force, although it has developed into a more complex 'Treaty System', with increased environmental provisions. The number of signatories now exceeds 50, with 29 of these (as of 2015) considered 'Consultative Parties' – that is, they maintain a significant scientific presence on the continent (something beyond the means of many developing nations) and have decision-making rights at annual meetings. The political landscape of Antarctica has become much more complex, with a far greater diversity of state actors, commercial interests (around tourism, bioprospecting and potential mineral resources) and NGOs such as Greenpeace.

During these changes, Amundsen-Scott South Pole Station has been continually upgraded and expanded. The Antarctic Treaty has changed the nature of the politics – Siple's frank nationalism would be naive in today's climate – but has not stopped the politicking. A report to Congress by the Office of Management and Budget in 1983 stated that the South Pole is 'symbolically and politically . . . the most important location for a U.S. station'.[17] With the Dome Station becoming increasingly less viable in the 1990s due to accumulation of ice, the spectre arose of having to abandon the station if it were not rebuilt. 'The costs could be substantial', wrote Frank G. Klotz, an airforce lieutenant colonel, in *America on the Ice*. 'Nevertheless, the United States must remain at this politically significant site if it is at all serious about exercising a major say in Antarctic affairs in the years ahead.'[18] A Presidential Decision Directive in 1996 stated baldly that

> United States presence at the South Pole Station demonstrates United States commitment to assert its rights in Antarctica, its basis of claim, and its commitment to conduct cutting edge scientific research there. Abandonment of the Station would create a vacuum and likely result in a scramble to occupy the site, to the detriment of our position as well as to the stability of the Treaty system.[19]

In the same year, the Undersecretary of State in the Clinton administration, Tim Wirth, similarly maintained the political high

Greenpeace blockade an airstrip site at Durmont d'Urville, Antarctica.

ground while asserting a United States presence: 'If we weren't at the South Pole, there would be a mad scramble for territory . . . We're the only country that can manage the logistics in that extraordinary place . . . We have to maintain this presence to maintain the continent's neutrality.'[20] In 1997 Congress approved President Clinton's request to begin building a new station, solidifying U.S. occupation of the Pole. While scientists and tourists of many different nations visit the Pole, and many current research programmes based there are international collaborations, the station nonetheless functions as an ongoing demonstration of specific U.S. power. Its pivotal position, sitting in six claimed territories at once, although neutral from one perspective, is from another a blatant statement of the nation's 'right to go anywhere and everywhere'.[21]

Contemporary political debates over the Antarctic, revolving around issues such as climate change and melting ice, potential extraction of mineral resources (currently banned by the Antarctic Treaty System), the intentions of new global powers such as China and India, and the impact of tourism, rarely explicitly involve the Geographic Pole, sitting on miles of ice in the interior of the continent. Occasionally, however, an event will set off a wave of interest about the prime position of the U.S. One trigger point was the construction of the 'South Pole Traverse', a compacted

The U.S. South Pole Station has a snow-packed skiway so that it can be serviced by ski-equipped planes such as this LC-130.

snow route for tractor convoys carrying materials and fuel from McMurdo Station to the Pole. The media quickly dubbed it a 'road' or even 'super highway'. While most objections were environmental, there was a particular sense of umbrage at the U.S. riding roughshod (so to speak) over the pristine icescape. 'Is this the beginning of the end for the last great wilderness?' asked the *Guardian* newspaper on hearing of the proposal, relating a British adventurer's experience of arriving at his destination to find a gift shop and 'a large stars and stripes marking the fact that the U.S. now controls the south pole'.[22]

The three other poles occupied in the IGY have seen diverse fates. Given the shifting nature of the Magnetic South Pole, the French station near there, Charcot, was a small, temporary affair: three men at a time occupied the base until it was abandoned at the end of the IGY. Another coastal French IGY station, Dumont d'Urville, became a permanent base. Vostok Station on the Geomagnetic South Pole – the most prominent of Russia's five permanent Antarctic bases – has remained occupied. Following the collapse of the Soviet Union, however, its future looked shaky; the base closed several times over winter due to an inability to provide fuel and resupplies and had to rely on U.S. emergency support to ensure the safety of personnel. 'Russia no longer considers its Antarctic bases politically important', reported the *New York Times* when Vostok was closed in the winter of 1994, although the Russian programme pointed to climatic conditions rather than lack of political commitment.[23] While the ever-restless Geomagnetic South Pole has slipped away over the station's half-century history and is now hundreds of miles away, the discovery of Lake Vostok – an enormous subglacial lake about 4 km (2.5 miles) beneath the base – has opened up an important area of research.

For relatively new players on the Antarctic political stage, the prime symbolic position is unavailable. But, ironically, the politics of climate change have led to a change in 'prestige locations' in the Antarctic. Interest is now focusing on the vertical rather than the horizontal – drilling down into the ice, not travelling across it. For this reason, high points in the continent have become important places – something that has benefited Vostok's scientific programme. The 'humps' in the ice plateau known as 'domes' are crucial – with the turn of the twenty-first century, domes seem to have become the new poles. Japan's Dome Fuji Station (at Dome F) was established in 1995; a decade later, a joint French and Italian station, Concordia, was built on Dome C. Four years after that, China opened Kunlun Station (its third on the continent) on Dome A, the highest and probably coldest station on the continent – an impressive logistical achievement that reflects and reinforces China's emergence as a political power, in Antarctica as in the rest of the globe.

Stations high in Antarctica's interior are ideal for glaciological, astronomical and atmospheric work. At Dome C, ice cores have been retrieved at a depth of 3,200 m (10,500 feet), revealing data from 800,000 years ago. At the higher Dome A, where snowfall is less and the ice reveals more data for the same depth, researchers are hoping to push back to 1.5 million years.[24] Even here, despite the evident usefulness of such data for human

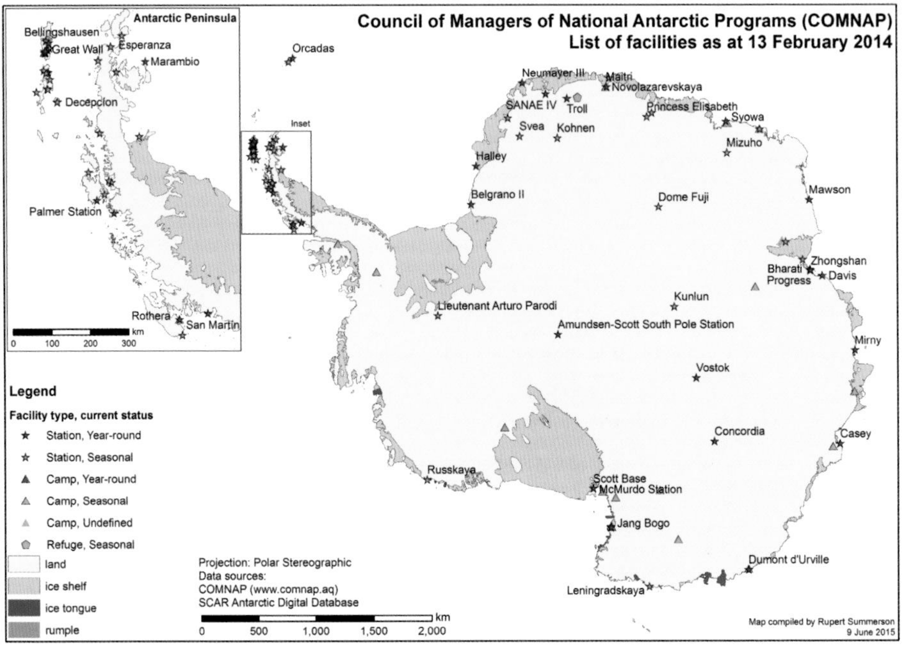

Map showing Antarctic stations and other facilities in 2014.

Bust of Lenin atop the buried Russian station at the Pole of Inaccessibility, 2008.

knowledge of the planet's history and ability to predict its future, it is hard not to sense political one-upmanship in the 'race' to see which nation or group of nations can dig deepest, peer back furthest.

One of the most telling images of polar politics, and a reminder of the Cold War roots of the Antarctic Treaty, shows the fate of the Soviet IGY base Polyus Nedostupnosti (Pole of Inaccessibility), established at 82°S, 55°E. The meteorological station was inhabited for a couple of weeks in late 1958 before being abandoned to the elements.[25] Unsurprisingly, it was considered too inaccessible for long-term habitation. Over the next half-century, it was visited very rarely, and when a private guided expedition arrived there in 2007, no one had reached the spot for almost two decades. The buildings, not unexpectedly, were covered by ice, but something remained poking up above it: approaching their destination, the adventurers saw a 'black dot' marking the white plateau, the only visible sign of the base. As they came closer, it resolved itself: it was a bust of Lenin.[26]

9 Pictures of Nothingness

In late 1956, when construction of the first South Pole station was about to get under way, a cartoon appeared in *Parade*, a widely read U.S. Sunday magazine: it showed a fur-clad expeditioner with a camera, against a uniformly white background shading into blank sky, instructing his subject, another fur-clad expeditioner: 'Now let's get one of you standing over there.'[1] The cartoon neatly encapsulates the aesthetic problem facing the visual artist at the Pole, at least in the popular imagination: what is there to see?

The continent's coastal regions and ice-strewn waters, first encountered in the late eighteenth and nineteenth centuries, with their impressive icebergs, calving glaciers, plentiful animal life and rocky edges, fitted fairly readily into existing aesthetic approaches, whether these came out of a natural history tradition or the developing conventions of the Picturesque and the Sublime. George Forster, a naturalist on James Cook's Antarctic circumnavigation in the late eighteenth century, drew on a proto-Romantic aesthetic in his single Antarctic image *The Ice Islands*, painted in gouache.[2] However, the expedition artist, William Hodges, seems to have been underwhelmed, artistically at least, by his Antarctic encounter. While he produced the first paintings of the region – five watercolours – this was far fewer than he created on other legs of the journey, and none of them was later worked up as an oil: 'One can only assume Hodges did not think the ice of the Antarctic Ocean was a suitable subject for a major painting.'[3] Later sea voyages, such as those led by Charles Wilkes and James Clark

Cartoon by David Huffine, *Parade* magazine, 1956.

Huffine
"Now let's get one of you standing over there."

Ross, generated artworks and illustrations in the naturalistic tradition, 'bringing the Antarctic coast into the visual imagination of Western civilization without seriously challenging [established] techniques and without suggesting that Antarctica was, for the visual arts, anything unique'.[4] Not all Antarctic art of this early period, however, was produced by those who had seen the continent: some of the best-known images of the region were the Gothic illustrations of an 1875 edition of Coleridge's poem 'The Rime of the Ancient Mariner', created by the popular French artist Gustave Doré, whose 'farthest south' at this point was a tour of Spain.[5]

Since Cook's time, fewer than 300 visual artists, according to one estimate, have visited Antarctica.[6] They have produced a large and varied body of art, including painting and photography in a diverse range of traditions, installation art, sculpture and fine art objects in the form of jewellery, glass and porcelain. Whole books have been written on the topic, and numerous exhibitions held. Most Antarctic art, however, responds to its coastal regions, with more recent artworks engaging particularly with scientific data and climate change. The interior plateau poses its own set of challenges: first, as an artist, how to get there; second, how to work in its conditions; and third, how to develop an artistic language equipped to respond to – or perhaps to challenge stereotypes of – its scale and bareness.

For the first artist to reach the Pole, Scott's trusted companion Edward Wilson, the first challenge was already moot (returning was the issue); the second he had come to terms with on an earlier, unsuccessful polar journey during the *Discovery* expedition; and the third would in one sense have been welcome. The problem was that the Pole – the goal of many weeks of struggle and suffering – was not, in fact, bare when Wilson arrived. He thus made sketches of his own forestalment: Amundsen's black flag, first from a distance and then much closer; a cairn the Norwegian team had left; the tent they had left as a marker. These images joined many he had already made on the polar journey, and would continue to produce on his return. They were found in the polar party's tent along with the men's bodies, and a number are reproduced in the first edition of Scott's journals. As the expedition zoologist, concerned with creating accurate records of his surrounds as much as aesthetic responses, Wilson was highly experienced at sketching in Antarctica. He knew its hazards: the low temperatures would freeze the watercolours he liked to paint in, not to mention exposed fingers, so sketches needed to be made in pencil and worked up later, ideally in the comparative comfort of a hut.[7]

Kirsten Haydon, ice horizon brooch, 2012. Enamel, copper, photo transfer, reflector beads, silver, steel, 80 × 80 × 15 mm.

By Wilson's time, not only an artist but a photographer was a common inclusion in Antarctic expeditions. Among the

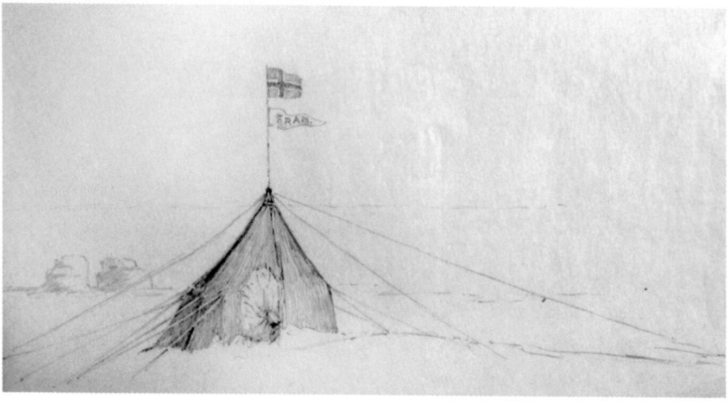

Edward Wilson's sketch of Amundsen's tent.

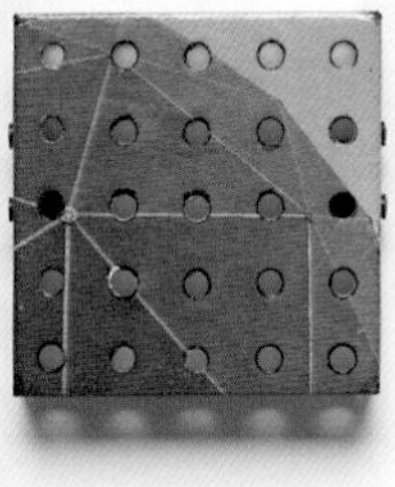

Kirsten Haydon, ice structure brooch, 2011. Enamel, reclaimed steel, photo transfer, silver, 65 × 65 × 12 mm.

continents, Antarctica is unique in that its exploration took place alongside the development of photography and cinematography, meaning that the shots taken of the continent were not preceded by any prior artistic images, indigenous or imported. The oceanographic *Challenger* expedition (1872–6) captured the first photographs of Antarctic icebergs and a Dundee whaling expedition in 1892–3 took the first of Antarctic land.[8] The earliest human settlement of the continent – the huts built by Carsten Borchgrevink's *Southern Cross* expedition in 1899 – included a darkroom, and it was this expedition that took the first photograph *on* the continent: a British flag.[9] Photographs had several uses: they served as records of achievements; encoded information about the topography and environment; provided a leisure activity for expeditioners, who sometimes brought their own cameras; and could be used in vital post-expedition publicity, such as newspapers and lectures. Ernest Shackleton's *Nimrod* expedition (1907–9) included at least fifteen still cameras – cumbersome but high-quality ones that used glass plates and smaller, more portable ones that took advantage of the newer technology of roll-film.[10] Shackleton – who had served as photographer on Scott's first attempt at the Pole – brought one of the former, along with 36 plates, on his own sledging journey towards the Pole, and it was used to take a photograph of his 'farthest south'.[11] Like the artist, the Antarctic photographer faced numerous challenges in the environment, including the weather conditions, the long periods of darkness during winter, the reaction of the equipment to the cold, the need to wear only one pair of gloves to work the camera, and the long exposure times that required subjects to stay painfully still. These problems meant that photography did not automatically replace art in Antarctica as a means of visual record.[12]

Training and equipment from a prominent Norwegian photographer formed part of the preparations for Amundsen's expedition, but in the end the official camera was damaged and the polar party had to rely on the personal camera belonging to Olav Bjaaland for its visual record of the journey.[13] Thus as an image-maker as well as an explorer Wilson was forestalled – by a portable Kodak. On the southward journey Amundsen's team

Motorer.

H. P. Andresen & Co.,

Tidens Tegn

Nr. 134. | Utkommer hver morgen. | Kristiania, torsdag 16. mai 1912. | Redigert av O. Thommessen. | 3. aarg.

Tidens Tegn

508

annoncer om kjøp og salg av eiendomme har „Tidens Tegn" hat fra 1—15 mai. Uaglet „Tidens Tegn" bare har virket et par aar, regnes det med rette blandt de allerførste av vore avertissementsblade. Kun et av vore ældre dagblade har flere eiendomsannoncer end „Tidens Tegn". Dets tilgang paa annoncer er stadig stigende. „Tidens Tegn" læses jo av alle, har av alle vore politiske blade den jevneste utbredelse over det hele land, er av alle politiske dagblade nr. 1 i utbredelse utenfor og nr. 2 i Kristiania.

Faste eiendomme.

1058

Maskinskrivning.

Spedition Transport & Bugsering A-B.

De første fotografier fra sydpolsfærden.

Offentliggjøres samtidig i „Tidens Tegn" og „Aftenposten".

Paa polen den 14. december 1911. Amundsen tar en observation ved hjælp av kunstig horisont.

Advokat Rieber-Mohns Kontor er lukket 17de Mai.

Centralbanken for Norge.
Fondsavdeling.
Panserhvelv.
Boxavdeling.
Formuesforvaltning.

Roald Amundsen
Oscar Mathisen
Lauritz Bergendahl

WANDERER

HANS ERICHSEN, Nytorvet 5.

Over Gjævelens ...

Centralvarmeanlæg

E. Sunde & Co.

This Norwegian newspaper article from May 1912 boasts the first photographs from Amundsen's expedition.

'photographed each other in "picturesque attitudes"', but the now iconic image shot by Bjaaland shows the team more reverential, hats off, side-on in a rough line beginning with their leader, looking up at their flag.[14] This is 'not merely a picture of someone somewhere', writes Harald Østgaard Lund, who curates the picture collection at the National Library of Norway: 'It is the ultimate mental image, the emblem of the proud, independent Norway, stamped, engraved, printed and reprinted again and again in books, magazines and films, on posters, postcards, stamps and packaging material.' The original negative has disappeared, and many versions – some hand-coloured – exist, with 'both the flag and Amundsen's belly' varying in slackness.[15]

Bjaaland's photograph of the rest of Amundsen's team at the South Pole. L–R: Amundsen, Hanssen, Hassel, Wisting.

In the same place a month or so later, while Wilson sketched, Birdie Bowers took photographs, including shots of his companions ranged disconsolately around the same tent. Scott's men seem dispersed and distracted. The British team took more formally posed shots next to their own flag – all five of them, standing in some versions and sitting in others; the string that Bowers pulled to trigger the shutter is just visible in some reproductions. Having received lessons earlier from the official expedition photographer (the first in Antarctica) Herbert Ponting, Scott himself took many of the photographs on other stages of the journey.[16] Ponting was back at the base. He and his heavy equipment could not travel more than the first two days of the journey, and anyway, Scott had reassured him, there would not be

Bowers's photograph of the rest of Scott's party ranged around Amundsen's tent. L–R: Scott, Oates, Wilson, Evans.

much to photograph on the plateau except 'boundless, featureless ice, with the long caravan stringing out towards the horizon'.[17] As it turned out, despite Ponting's fine photographic record of the expedition, the 'selfies' taken by the downcast men at the Pole have become its visual emblem.

Amundsen and Scott also brought cinematograph (moving film) cameras, as did other expedition leaders such as Shackleton, Charcot, Mawson, Shirase and even Borchgrevink in the very late nineteenth century. These cameras too could not come on polar journeys. For Amundsen, departing for the Pole, the last sign of civilization was the surreal sight of his endeavour being recorded for posterity: one of the men staying at the base turned the crank of the cinematograph, the machine disappearing below the horizon as the team passed over a ridge.[18] Ponting had learned the new technology for Scott's expedition, and showed numerous versions of the resulting film over his lifetime, to gradually diminishing audiences. His inability to capture the polar journey *was* significant: the narrative is marred by the gaping hole in its middle, which Ponting could fill only with pre-enactments, illustrations, maps, stills, intertitles and (in the last version) voice-overs. Frank Hurley, another important early Antarctic photographer and cinematographer, suffered a similar problem when Shackleton's

This illustration from a Norwegian newspaper shows Amundsen lecturing to a large home crowd in September 1912, displaying images from his expedition.

The *Terra Nova* expedition photographer Herbert Ponting with telephoto apparatus.

attempt to cross the continent via the Pole (the Imperial Trans-Antarctic Expedition of 1914–17) went awry before it even reached land. The dramatic footage of the ice-crushed *Endurance* sinking in the Weddell Sea was some consolation, but Hurley nonetheless appended some footage of animals on the sub-antarctic island of South Georgia, shot on a separate trip, to keep the crowds happy.

These early images of Antarctica were produced at a time when the artistic world was in transition, moving away from established conventions of visual representation and towards the experimentation, formal abstraction and expression of internal states of mind characteristic of modernism. The seminal discussion of Antarctic art in Stephen Pyne's *The Ice* emphasizes the irony that Antarctica's 'abstractions, minimalism, and abolished perspective' failed to engage the modernist artists best equipped to handle these challenges. Modernists' interest, Pyne notes, was focused elsewhere; additionally, there was the challenge of travelling to the plateau after the 'Heroic Age' had waned.[19] Anyone wanting immediate experience at the Pole, whether artist or scientist, had to wait for several decades after Wilson had departed.

This hiatus meant that, apart from the aerial survey photographs taken on Richard Byrd's overflight of 1929 – some of which were reproduced in the expedition account, *Little America* (1931) – any new visual representations of the Pole in the interim had to borrow from other icy landscapes. The film *Scott of the Antarctic* (1948) heavily referenced Ponting's work and included some footage (without actors) taken in the Antarctic Peninsula, but its icy action scenes were shot in Switzerland and (somewhat ironically) Norway.[20] The film included a score by the renowned British composer Ralph Vaughan Williams, later revised as his *Sinfonia antarctica*. (Antarctic music – including film scores – has its own substantial history, with contributions by well-known composers such as Peter Maxwell Davies, Nigel Westlake and Ennio Morricone.)

It was only with the establishment of the U.S. base in the later 1950s that visual artists were again able to travel to 90 degrees south. They had to do so as guests of the U.S. military, as there was no other means of travel for those not wanting to sledge across the ice. The first painting produced outdoors at the Pole was by an official Navy artist, 70-year-old Arthur Beaumont. Already accustomed to polar conditions from his artistic assignment in the Arctic, Beaumont stayed at the South Pole station for a week in the summer of 1960–61, working outside by mixing his watercolour paints with torpedo alcohol.[21] His *South Pole Station* shows a surprisingly colourful and crowded Pole, dominated by the radar tracking station for weather balloons, with the stripy ceremonial marker attached to a U.S. flag off-centre in the foreground, and seemingly undulating hills in the distance.

Independent visual artists as well as those officially employed by the Navy travelled to the Pole in its early years of settlement. The Swiss photographer Emil Schulthess spent time at several U.S. Antarctic bases over the 1958–9 summer season, producing a book entitled simply *Antarctica* (1960). Although unable to visit the Pole, he flew over it, taking aerial shots of the year-old station and the cargo-dropping process. Later, he gave a fish-eye camera to a naval sergeant with instructions to shoot long exposures pointing both up and down at the Pole. The upwards image tracked the path of the sun across the sky: 'surely', Schulthess claimed in his book, 'the first photographic record of the "southern end" of the axis of the earth'.[22] For Pyne, Schulthess as photojournalist is a 'successor to the heroic era', using new technology to conquer some of the plateau's challenges without departing from representational art.[23]

A very different visual artist arrived at the Pole five years later. Sidney Nolan – one of Australia's best-known painters – spent eight days in the continent together with writer Alan Moorehead as a guest of the U.S. Navy, including a trip to the Pole.[24] Nolan's visit was, according to William L. Fox, the point when modernism arrived on the continent: 'his paintings of glaciers [are] as much about the flow of his emotions as the ice'.[25] Nolan produced 68 paintings (mostly oils) from his time in Antarctica, based on now-missing photographs and watercolours made on site. The first images he produced were landscapes of the coast, conceived as 'a series of abstract configurations or densely knitted patterns'.[26] The Pole itself does not seem to have particularly interested Nolan, except to the extent that it informed the 'Explorer' figures that emerge halfway through his Antarctic series. Nolan's diary indicates that Scott's polar journey provided the specific inspiration behind *Camp*, in which two featureless men stand behind a tent with a Union Jack flying, the foreground a mess of shattered ice, the horizon one long grey-white block.[27] His generic explorers are 'vulnerable, isolated, sometimes brutalised. In places they are self-depreciating, ungainly and even slightly comic or absurd.'[28] Ironically, Nolan's modernist images of Antarctica, produced between his paintings of the doomed explorers of the Australian interior Burke and Wills and his famous images of the bushranger Ned Kelly, suggest the continent's similarity to the Australian desert as much as its alien otherness.[29]

By the time the influential American landscape photographer Eliot Porter reached the Pole in the mid-1970s, the old station had been replaced by the Dome, and the military by the National Science Foundation. The side-flap of Porter's collection *Antarctica*

Sidney Nolan, *Camp* (Captain Scott's 1912 South Pole Expedition), 1964, oil on hardboard.

(1978) promises 'such majestic images as the desolate South Pole', but in fact he conspicuously avoided the Pole itself, and shows comparatively little interest in the plateau. What for Schulthess was a 'fascinating endless snowscape' of which he could not tire was for Porter a 'dreary landscape'.[30] It features in his collection only when punctured by more traditionally spectacular mountains and nunataks. Porter had established his reputation as a wilderness photographer and frames his Antarctic collection in terms of potential environmental threat, describing the myriad 'predictable consequences of economic exploitation of the last untouched land'.[31] For the critic Elena Glasberg, it is Porter's desire to produce 'dramatic and anachronistic images of seemingly untouched nature' that led him to eschew the Pole: 'within the Porter aesthetic there would be nothing to see there but the significant evidence of U.S. colonization'.[32] At the same time, she argues, Porter's work, which packaged the continent for a U.S. audience in the same visual terms as the American west he had so famously photographed, 'marked the Antarctic as an object of U.S. concern, and possibly ownership'.[33] Where Nolan's art draws artistic connections with Australian deserts, then, Porter's joins Antarctica to American landscapes: everyone, it seems, finds their own familiarity within strangeness.

For the Minnesotan Stuart Klipper, whose oeuvre displays a horizontal, wide-field and elemental aesthetic, the Antarctic plateau was an obvious fit. Some of his photographs of the far south are collected in his book *The Antarctic: From the Circle to the Pole* (2008). In his South Pole images, human traces disturb the otherwise confident sweep of the panorama. *The Geographic South Pole* – an image taken moments after Klipper first arrived at 90 degrees south – shows the familiar sign in the centre foreground dominated by a fluttering U.S. flag (itself cut off by the frame), with a series of marker flags visible in the vague whiteness behind, distracting the viewer from the central object. In *Spryte Tracks*, the imprint of a vehicle heading out into the faintly sastrugied plateau stops unaccountably just where a shaft of refracted sunlight penetrates the image, so it appears that the aliens so ubiquitous in Antarctic mythology have beamed up the machine. The U.S. Antarctic Program (USAP) evidently liked what it saw, because, after an initial trip south with a private sailing expedition, Klipper travelled with the Program to Antarctica five times between 1989 and 2000, making four separate visits to the Pole. Having taken more than 10,000 Antarctic images, Klipper has produced 'by far the largest and farthest-ranging body of visual work by one person in this area'.[34]

By the late twentieth century the USAP's intermittent support of particular artists and writers wishing to travel to the South Pole and its other stations had developed into a systematic programme,

Stuart Klipper, *The Geographic South Pole* (1989).

minuscule compared to the scientific programme but with its own application process and criteria. While even into the twenty-first century the U.S., like other nations, has tended to send 'traditional painters or straight-ahead nature and landscape photographers' south, room opened for more experimental approaches.[35] And although the Artists and Writers Program in one sense acts as the 'cultural wing' (to use Glasberg's term[36]) of broader U.S. activities in the region, effectively excluding projects that are obviously hostile to this effort, work that complicates or resists official discourse and representation nevertheless emerges.

One example is the photography of An-My Lê, a political refugee to the U.S. from the Vietnam War best known for her work dealing with war and military activities. Her aim in travelling to Antarctica – she visited McMurdo as well as the Pole – was to look at the role of the military in providing science support (transport and logistics) in the USAP.[37] Lê's approach, however, is a long way from that of the official naval artists and photographers who were part of the program's early days. Her *Events Ashore* series, first exhibited in 2008, 'examine[s] intersecting themes of scientific exploration, military power, environmental crises, fantasies of empire and the vast ungovernable oceans that connect nations and continents'.[38] Alongside images of military activity around the globe, Lê placed photographs of Antarctic stations. Works such as *Abandoned Dome* and *Storage Berms at the South Pole* ignore the station's glamorous icons – the Ceremonial Pole, the new state-of-the-art station – in favour of discarded, marginal and utilitarian structures. Her 'vision of Antarctica', in Glasberg's analysis, refuses 'the overexposed, official view' of the continent as an exceptional place and instead positions it as 'a site in the global economy'.[39]

Most of the South Pole images produced by the Los Angeles photographer Connie Samaras also focus on human infrastructure, although her lines are cleaner and starker than Lê's, as befitting a project that she entitled (referencing science fiction writer Philip K. Dick) 'Vast Active Living Intelligence System: Photographing the South Pole'. Samaras has commented that 'It's very hard not to go Ansel Adams' when confronted with the plateau,[40] but she resists the urge. Her photographs of the half-finished new station (Samaras visited in 2004) present it in sections rather than as a whole – a series of detached, impenetrable boarded blocks on stilts.[41] Samaras's project was to investigate 'the liminal space between life support architecture and extreme environment'.[42] *Underneath Scott-Amundsen Station* does this quite literally, showing the area beneath the building designed to be scoured out by wind to prevent accumulating snow – the camera occupies the protective space that separates human artefact from encroaching ice. Samaras's photographs of the earlier stations, however, ironically inflect this image. In *Domes and Tunnels*, the NSF station is nearly swallowed by snow drift, and the promise of the brightly lit, glossily red, neatly symmetrical

An-My Lê, *Abandoned Dome, South Pole, Antarctica*, 2008. Archival pigment print. 101.5 × 143.5 cm

Dome Interior (Samaras mirrored the image) is undermined by the knowledge of its engulfment by ice. The aerially shot *Buried Fifties Station* shows a few just-discernible marks on the sastrugi-strewn plain. For all its jack-uppable, aerodynamic assurance, the newest station is not the end point of human occupation at the Pole, just the latest in an ongoing expendable series. Samaras felt 'a poetic relief' as she 'observed and documented the geological timeline indifferently erasing attempts to colonize the polar plateau'.[43]

Not all contemporary visual art dealing with the South Pole is created *at* the South Pole. Anne Noble has travelled to Antarctica three times, on a tourist cruise and with the New Zealand and U.S. national programmes, with the latter including a visit to the Pole. Even before this time, however, the photographs in her *Southern Lights* exhibition (2005) present Antarctica's symbolic centre in both playful and telling ways. These are not so much images of the South Pole as images of how humans make images

Connie Samaras, *Underneath Amundsen-Scott Station* from the exhibition *V.A.L.I.S.: Vast Active Living Intelligence System* (2005).

Connie Samaras, *Dome Interior* from the exhibition *V.A.L.I.S.: Vast Active Living Intelligence System* (2005).

of the South Pole. One shows a CD inscribed with the shape of the continent, a button in the middle labelled 'push' marking the place where the South Pole would be. Another offers a close-up of a children's blow-up globe, with the stopper at the Pole. A third shows a signpost indicating distances from the South Pole to major cities of the world – but the signpost is not at the Pole but in the Fuji Antarctic Museum in Nagoya, Japan. By selling copies of the images on jigsaws and postcards – her *Antarctic Collectibles* – Noble added another layer to her examination of the way in which representations of the continent are repackaged and circulated.

One representation to which artists seem to be repeatedly drawn is the famous set of photographs taken by Bowers at the Pole in 1912. Noble took one of these shots as an inspiration for a 're-photographic project'.[44] Her series of five images *Had We Lived* (2012) – photographs of a photograph – present the five men separately rather than together, each seeming to peer through a circle of soft, blurry light, obscured and yet caught in a spotlight. Although they continue to 'live' in the circulation of their images, the men in the individual portraits are divorced from both each other and the 'tale they had to tell', yet the viewer is invited to read their faces with an intimacy discouraged by the formality of the original shot. In the book/CD collaboration *These Rough Notes* (2012), which Noble produced together with the composer Norman Meehan and the poet Bill Manhire, these

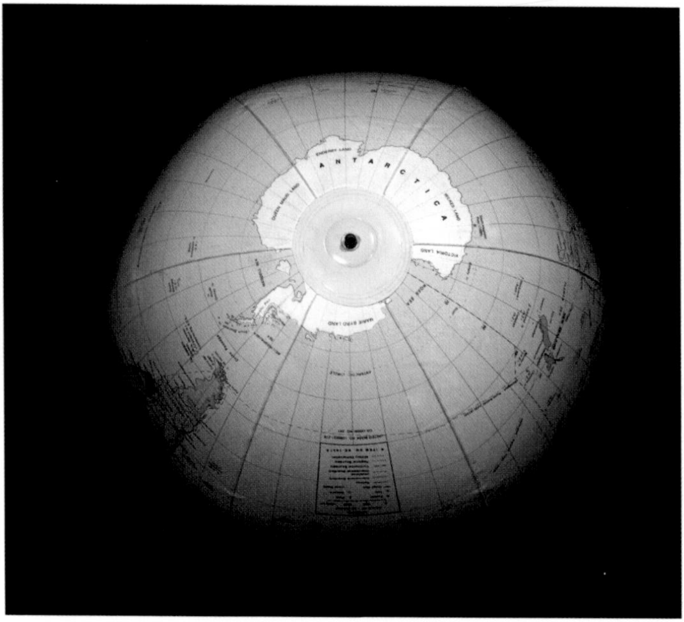

Anne Noble, *White Lantern* (2004).

images are juxtaposed with re-photographs of the Erebus air disaster of 1979, which dwarfs in scale and thus recontextualizes the polar tragedy, putting the focus on loss and memory rather than heroism and achievement. The British artist Paul Coldwell, in a series of images produced for his *Re-Imagining Scott* expedition (2013), also manipulates Bowers's images as a reflection upon memory and time passing. Coldwell took digital images of *Terra Nova* photographs – including those from the Pole – and reduced their visual information before printing them out and working on the surface with paint or gouache: 'My intention was to heighten the sense of surface so the viewer needed to look through this to the photograph beyond . . . too close and the image becomes unreadable, too far away and the image becomes lost.'[45]

Site-specific art is not easy in Antarctica, because of the weather conditions as well as the limited (if captive) audience, but it does have its own history there, recorded in photographs. In 2007 the Miami artist Xavier Cortada arranged 24 shoes around the Ceremonial Pole as one of a series of installations. Because longitude lines converge at the Pole, the shoes, although in a tight circle, were all at different longitudes. At each shoe, Cortada read a statement from a person affected by climate change elsewhere in the world at the same longitude.[46] It is tempting to wonder what the locals made of his efforts; as is sometimes noted in their accounts, writers and artists tend to be considered supernumerary in a place where accommodation is pushed to its limit.

Polies of course produce their own visual responses to place, as evidenced by the innumerable images available on the Internet. Samaras suggests that, given the relatively small number of visitors to the Pole, 'per capita it may be more photographed than Disney World'.[47] Polies also hold their own 'South Pole International Film Festival' (SPIFF) to display their efforts, some of which are accessible online, and (like the personnel of other Antarctic stations) they can enter the larger film festival organized by McMurdo base. Unsurprisingly in an environment where outdoor activities are highly constrained, the station includes its own arts and craft room. Occasionally, a home-grown

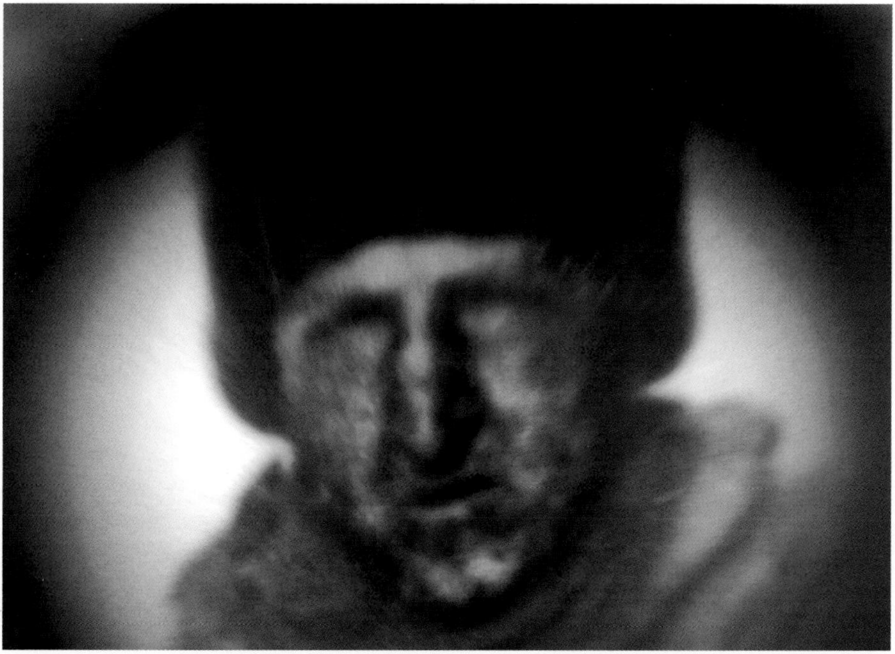

Anne Noble, *Had We Lived . . . #2 (Bowers)* (2012).

'Spoolhenge' in early September 2013: a stack of spools from cables used for the IceCube detector, illuminated from behind by the rising sun with a faint aurora visible on the right.

Paul Coldwell, *At the Pole 1*, 2013, ink gouache, enamel onto inkjet, 20 × 28 cm (produced for the exhibition *Re-Imagining Scott: Objects and Journeys*, Scott Polar Research Institute, Cambridge).

sculpture of sorts will appear, such as the appealing 'Spoolhenge': in a postmodern take on ancient astronomy, a series of stacked giant spools – some of which, according to online accounts, originally held the cables (miles long) attached to the IceCube neutrino detectors – became a line of cylindrical menhirs. Local and visiting artistic impulses meet in Noble's series of photographs of the object, *Spoolhenge Antarctica*, exhibited in 2008.

While still photography seems to have dominated artistic responses to it in recent years, the Pole is also the subject of numerous films and television documentaries and docudramas. Often it plays a small part in a bigger story: Werner Herzog's Antarctic documentary *Encounters at the End of the World* (2007), for example, includes a couple of brief segments at the Pole, which the director regretted was ever reached. 'At a cultural level', he reflects, the arrivals of Amundsen and Scott meant 'the end of adventure', which thereafter 'degenerated into absurd quests'. The Pole is the occasional setting of feature films, from the intriguing fictional documentary *The Forbidden Quest* (1993) to the unremarkable action thriller *Whiteout* (2009), and of television dramas – a 2008 episode of the hospital series *House*, evidently influenced by physician Jerri Nielsen's real-life emergency, features the eponymous medical genius attempting the long-distance diagnosis of a researcher at the Pole. Logistics and expense, however, mean that Antarctic drama is seldom filmed on site.

Visual representations of a place inevitably affect humans' relationship with that place, no matter how familiar it is from their everyday experience. When it comes to the South Pole, a place comparatively few people have ever directly seen, images become even more potent. The point is made humorously in the novelist Wolcott Gibbs's satire of the relationship between the press, publicity and polar exploration, *Bird Life at the Poles* (1931). In the novel the newspaper magnate 'Mr Herbst' (read Randolph Hearst) convinces a British explorer to lead an expedition to the South Pole and produce 400 press articles on his return. Before leaving, the explorers pose before a backdrop of snowy mountains borrowed from a Ziegfield ballet set. Questioning whether the image matches 'the idea people have of the South Pole', the expedition leader is informed that 'In this country . . . people think everything looks the way they see it in the Herbst papers.' In the twenty-first century most people still have to rely on others' representations for their visual image of the South Pole, but at least now there is a diverse range from which to choose.

10 Adventurers and Extreme Tourists

The arrival of the teams led by Amundsen and Scott at the South Pole in the summer of 1911–12 was the end point of a long-standing quest. In another sense, however, these expeditions marked a beginning: they were the first in a series of overland traverses to the Pole that now number well into the hundreds. Like the summit of Everest – the 'third Pole' – the South Pole retains its allure as the terminus of one of the world's most testing physical journeys. Yet, unlike Everest's peak, it is a destination safely and easily reached by those with sufficient funds: a well-established tour company can fly you there, feed you a fresh meal in a heated tent and put you up comfortably overnight, 'nice and warm' in your heavy-duty sleeping bag.[1]

Where does the category of 'explorer' blur into 'adventurer' or even 'extreme tourist'? Robert Headland, in his comprehensive list of Antarctic expeditions, points to the burgeoning in the last decade of the twentieth century of 'unprecedented activities, such as re-enactment of selected aspects of "heroic age" expeditions, long running races, parachute jumps, ballooning, surfing, diving and kayaking contests, use of snow-boards, various endurance feats, and similar stunts'. Sniffily, but with some justification, he refuses to apply the word 'exploration' to such 'contriving [of] adventures for claims of alleged record breaking and the like'.[2]

Historically speaking, however, the line is not always easy to draw.[3] The wealthy Lawrence Oates offered to donate £1,000 to Scott's second expedition if he could be a member. Given that one modern researcher defines Antarctic tourism as 'the commercial (for profit) transport (including accommodation and catering) of nongovernment travelers to and from Antarctica for the purpose of pleasure', Oates might – at a stretch – be considered the first tourist to the South Pole.[4] Scott's expedition was not a moneymaking venture but it was a private undertaking, and Oates did effectively pay to be transported to the continent, which presumably represented various pleasures for him, although these were diminishing rapidly by the time he reached the Pole. Early twentieth-century commentators certainly saw the permeability of the border between explorer and tourist. In Wolcott Gibbs's Antarctic exploration satire *Bird Life at the Pole*, a South Polar expedition finds itself forestalled at a crucial moment by a group from 'Popular Polar Tours'.

These days the line between expeditioner and tourist is even less clear. Most private expeditions to the Pole in the last few decades have relied on a commercial operator for logistical support. And commentators have noted that some modern definitions of tourism would class most scientists and other personnel in Antarctica as tourists simply because their stays are so

Athletes and adventure tourists fly to 80 degrees south to take part in the annual Antarctic Ice Marathon.

short.[5] In a continent where no one lives permanently, and no one can last long without outside support, everyone is, potentially, a tourist.

What are the attractions of the South Pole as a travel destination, now that it is an inhabited place, with a 'road' joining it to McMurdo Station on the coast? For some, there is the personal challenge of making what continues to be, despite innovations in equipment and clothing, and the availability of support and rescue services, an extremely arduous and sometimes dangerous journey. The prominent adventurer Ranulph Fiennes's reaction to reaching the Pole in late 1980 is a case in point. As part of the Transglobe Expedition (which followed one of the 'great circles' of longitude through both poles using surface transport only), he and two others trekked across Antarctica from the edge of Dronning Maud Land – the first transcontinental journey since the Fuchs-Hillary expedition of the 1950s. On arrival at his southernmost destination, Fiennes was 'exhausted, relieved, and perhaps a little confused by what I found there . . . a set piece of prefabricated huts, oil drums, woollen socks, and bearded men sustained by a fug of central heating and obscure scientific data'. The adventurers ate in the station canteen, helping out by washing up and refilling the ice cream machine. Fiennes was himself not averse to the conveniences of modern technology: he had ridden a skidoo to the Pole, with an aircraft dropping supplies. But the bathetic conclusion to this leg of his journey in no way detracted from his reverence for the place:

The confused explorers of Gibbs's *Bird Life at the Pole* (1931) are forestalled by an early tourist group.

> Although remote, and out of reach of most, there is something of the South Pole in the hearts of all of us. It's that place to harbour desire and aspiration, a home for that something that calls out to us, urging the human spirit to meet the challenge and the freedom of the wilderness.[6]

Personal challenge, along with a sense of deep, meditative pleasure in simply being on and travelling across the plateau, is central to the accounts of many polar journeys, whether they are made by experienced professional adventurers like Fiennes or by self-professed burnt-out urbanites, such as Catherine Hartley. But there are further attractions. For some, as Headland notes, the opportunity of a polar 'first' is irresistible. Hartley, along with a companion, was the first British woman to walk to the Pole. Precedence can be based on identity – gender, race, nationality, age, familial relations (parent/child or sibling teams), disability; on the means of travel – use of equipment or vehicles, degree of support, speed, ability to travel solo; and on the route travelled – whether the journey is simply to the Pole or a return journey, a continental crossing, or in combination with other 'polar' journeys (North Pole and Everest); and permutations of any of these. The Belgian Dixie Dansercoer, who has himself notched up quite a few firsts, worries in his guidebook for potential Arctic and Antarctic adventurers about the 'world of polar expeditions . . . becoming simply a competitive sport'.[7]

Conversely, there is the pleasure of repeating the achievements of others. Nostalgia, rather than precedence, here becomes

Adventure skiers nearing the South Pole after travelling from the coast.

the main theme, with expeditions recreating, with varying degrees of attempted authenticity, the seminal journeys of the 'Heroic Era'. The possibility of vindicating a favoured explorer or shedding light through direct experience on a controversial historical point is an added bonus.

Lastly, for those unable or unwilling to travel under their own steam, there is nonetheless kudos – as well as, no doubt, a sense of personal satisfaction – in simply being at a location that was, not much more than a century ago, out of reach of humanity, and is still, on a global scale, a very remote and unvisited place. Since 1988 it has been possible – if expensive – to pay to be transported to the Pole as a tourist. There is not a great deal to do once you arrive, but this is no real deterrent; perhaps the one thing better than being at the Pole is being able to say you have been there. Given that walking or skiing from the coast – or for any significant distance in the Antarctic conditions – is beyond the power of many of us, a commercial tourist flight is the obvious means to achieve a physical presence at 90 south. Even those working at the Pole are not immune to the pleasure of the boast of having *been* – even better, *lived* – there. They 'are conscious of and enjoy their status at the most famous location on the continent', but their pleasure is hampered by the fact that 'the location itself generates the fame, more than anyone working there or anything that happens there.'[8] In this sense Polies have something of the tourist about them, too.

In the blurry continuum between South Polar exploring and adventuring, a possible transition point is the Commonwealth Trans-Antarctic Expedition of the late 1950s. After this time, with a scientific base established and constantly resupplied at the Pole, and various national programmes conducting scientific and exploratory activities in the continent's interior, private expeditioners could be more accurately classed as adventurers. Since 1957 polar travellers have known that, having arrived at the Pole, they do not have to turn around and trudge back, but can always, whether by choice or due to an emergency, be evacuated by plane. This knowledge makes a big difference to the journey (not to mention the load that needs to be pulled).

However, this situation creates its own problems. The relationship between national programmes and private expeditions has never been cosy. Although the former will grudgingly provide support and rescue services if required, they do not encourage independent activity on the continent, which could potentially be a significant drain on their time and resources. A classic example of a clash between private adventurers and the U.S. Antarctic Program (USAP) is the 'Footsteps of Scott' expedition. Adventurers Roger Mear, Robert Swan and Gareth Wood followed the path of Scott's polar party, wintering at Cape Evans in 1985 before departing for the Pole, like Scott's team, in early November. They hauled sledges to the Pole – a distance of around 1,400 km (900 miles) – with no radio contact and no outside assistance, arriving about a week earlier than Scott had. They had arranged secretly for a pilot to pick them up from the Pole, but things went awry when their expedition ship sank off Cape Evans on the day they reached their southern target. In their account of the journey, their biggest adversary was not this misfortune or the hostile environment, but rather the USAP, which required them to be evacuated from the Pole on one of its own aircraft. While the individual workers at the Pole clapped and cheered them as they arrived, official representatives were far from welcoming: 'I have nothing against you people personally, but you were warned. We made it clear before . . . There is no place in the Antarctic for adventures such as yours'.[9] It remains U.S. policy that private polar travellers cannot expect to be taken in, fed or even welcomed at Amundsen-Scott Station: 'Tourists aglow from having arrived at the South Pole are met by management with a unique official courtesy that borders on scorn, and with indifference by Pole citizens.'[10]

The earliest of South Polar adventurers did not follow in the footsteps of Amundsen and Scott but rather in the contrails of Richard Byrd. The year 1965 saw the first flight over the Pole by a private plane: sponsored by the aircraft and spacecraft manufacturing company Rockwell-Standard, a Flying Tigers jet, *The Pole Cat*, travelled a route that also took in the North Pole. In early 1970 the Norwegians Thor Tjøntveit and Einar Pedersen flew a Cessna aeroplane from New Zealand, via McMurdo, to the South Pole, and on to Chile. At almost exactly the same time the American Max Conrad, the so-called Flying Grandfather, piloted a twin-engined plane along the same initial route. He just beat the Norwegians, gaining the record for the first civilian flight to arrive at the Pole, but not the first to return: he crashed when taking off. His plane, *The White Penguin*, was abandoned at the Pole, and remains there; Conrad (67 at the time) was flown out care of the USAP. Over the next couple of decades, several more American aviators flew over the South Pole as part of record-breaking journeys taking in both poles: Elgen Long, Brooke Knapp (the first woman to pilot a plane on a bi-polar journey) and Richard Norton. Flying *over* the Pole had the advantage of avoiding the lukewarm official reception offered to those who landed: 'a cup of coffee represented the sum total of American generosity for the tired flyer at the South Pole'.[11]

The quintessential polar journey remained, however, an overland haul – walking, skiing, in a small group or alone, perhaps with dogs, preferably with minimal support and mechanical help. It was inevitable that the 'Footsteps of Scott' expedition would be followed by more adventurers tracing the paths of 'Heroic Era' journeys. The 'Ninety Degrees South' expedition, led by the Norwegian glaciologist Monica Kristensen, aimed to take Amundsen's route to the Pole. Using dog teams, they left from the Bay of Whales at about the same time that Mear and his companions were trudging over the plateau. Suffering from a late start and comparatively slow progress, the expedition was forced to turn back at around 86 degrees south; if they had achieved their goal, Kristensen would have been the first woman to reach the Pole over land. As it turned out, this first went to two members of the earliest tourist traverse, Shirley Metz and Victoria Murden, part of a group who arrived at the Pole in early 1989. Kristensen led expeditions to the South Pole several more times in the early 1990s, in search of Amundsen's buried tent, but the quest ended in tragedy when a team member plunged to his death in a crevasse.

If Amundsen's and Scott's footsteps were being retraced, then so too, naturally, were Shackleton's. The renowned South Tyrolean mountaineer Reinhold Messner, together with the

German Arved Fuchs, took on the challenge of completing a transcontinental crossing – the task that Shackleton had to abandon in 1915 when his ship, the *Endurance*, famously sank in the Weddell Sea. Messner and Fuchs used two airdropped resupply depots, but no dogs or motorized vehicles. Unable to leave, as planned, from the outer edge of the Ronne Ice Shelf, they started from a point 500 km (311 miles) inside the shelf in mid-November 1989, reaching the Pole on New Year's Eve, and arriving at Ross Island the following February. At the same time another continental crossing was taking place: the highly publicized International Trans-Antarctica Expedition, made up of six men from six different countries. The route they chose was far longer than Messner's – 6,400 km (3,975 miles), taking them through five different stations – and required multiple airdropped supplies and refreshment of the dog teams. The expedition left in the middle of the Antarctic winter and took 213 days to complete the journey.[12]

Both Messner's team and the Trans-Antarctica Expedition were keen to raise awareness about Antarctica's endangered future, at a time when national programmes were debating the possibility of mining in the continent and environmental organizations were promoting the alternative idea of a World Park. The 1991 'Madrid Protocol' introduced a range of environmental policies, including the exclusion of sledge dogs from the continent; the final dogs were removed in early 1994. One of the last private expeditions to use them inadvertently demonstrated the wisdom of the policy: when the remarkable 87-year-old Norman D. Vaughan, expert dog-driver and veteran of Byrd's 1928–30 South Polar expedition, flew into the continent in late 1993 to climb the mountain named after him, the plane crashed and several of his dogs escaped, to unknown fates (paw prints were seen many miles away).[13] He succeeded, presumably sans dogs, a year later. With the days of using dog teams at an end, a new limitation was placed on expeditions, especially those attempting to replicate the 'Heroic' experience.

There were, however, many other modes of getting to the Pole, some less obvious than others. In early 1992 the Japanese

Shinji Kazama at the South Pole.

adventurer Shinji Kazama reached the South Pole on a modified Yamaha motorcycle, having previously conquered the North Pole and several iconic mountains by the same means. His 24-day trip – made with support from a team on snowmobiles – set an overland speed record for a South Pole traverse (it had taken Hillary's tractors 82 days). It was well and truly beaten, however, by a group of six-wheeled 'Snow Bugs' used in the Russian Millennium Expedition, and then by a modified six-wheel-drive Ford Van in 2005, which took just less than three days to make the journey. The first bio-fuelled vehicle journey to the Pole – part of a round trip – was completed in late 2010, demonstrating the capabilities of the technology. Non-motorized traverses also proliferated, with adventurers trying out parasails, kite-skis and bicycles for all or parts of the journey.

For some adventurers, a particular challenge was located in their own bodies. Cato Pedersen, a Norwegian Paralympic medallist who has no arms, skied to the Pole in 1994 with two companions, hauling his own load and using a prosthetic right arm to hold a ski-pole. Alan Lock, near-blind, made the journey in 2012. The paraplegic Grant Korgan used a device called a 'sit-ski' to traverse roughly the last degree to the Pole on the exact centenary of Scott's arrival. In late 2013 the British royal Prince Harry joined a group of wounded servicemen and -women who walked 200 km (124 miles) to the Pole, having made a similar journey in the Arctic; a documentary of the event, *Harry's South Pole Heroes*, appeared on British television shortly afterwards. Raising money or awareness for charities and causes – along with continual blogging about the adventure for the benefit of supporters – has become a common component of polar endeavour in the twenty-first century.

Of course, polar traverses – and polar tourism of any kind – are limited to the small segment of the world's population that has the means (or the ability to raise the funds) to pay for the travel. As a result, South Polar adventurism and tourism tends to be skewed towards particular demographics, a realization that in itself generates new 'firsts'. For example, Sibusiso Vilane, brought up in a poor rural community in Swaziland, became 'the first black African to walk unassisted to the South Pole' in early 2008, raising money for disadvantaged African children.[14]

For another set of adventurers, the challenge lies in paring down the journey as far as possible. Expeditions are classed according to how much help the traveller receives: 'unassisted' means that no external source of power (such as dogs, wind or motorized vehicle) is used; 'unsupported' means that there are no resupplies – the traveller carries all food and equipment for the journey. The first person to make a successful unassisted and unsupported solo traverse to the South Pole was the Norwegian Erling Kagge, in 1993. The following year his compatriot Liv Arnesen became the second person (and first woman) to achieve this, writing up her experiences in a book titled (in English translation) *Good Girls Do Not Ski to the South Pole.* A third Norwegian, Børge Ousland, passed through the Pole on the first solo continental crossing in 1996, although he was assisted by parasail.

These solo adventurers, self-sufficient and moving through a minimalist landscape, report a sense of existential plenitude as they go deeper into the journey. Kagge wrote of his endeavour: 'It is an absurd thing to do, but love makes you blind. I fell in love with the idea of skiing into a white nothingness, with everything I would need for an entire expedition on my sledge, and, as I wrote in my diary, to be able to feel that "Past and future are of no interest. I am living more and more in the present."'[15] For Ousland, the experience created 'a state of meditation where you reach levels inside you that you did not know existed' and Arnesen reported 'the feeling of being at one with nature – of knowing why I was there, what life is, who I am'.[16]

For others, historical concerns are paramount. The centenaries of the polar journeys of Shackleton, Amundsen and Scott provoked, unsurprisingly, a flurry of expeditions, some of them recreating aspects of the original events. In 2008 the Matrix Shackleton Centenary Expedition arrived at the Pole, all of the members descendants of the *Nimrod* expedition during which a team led by Shackleton made the decision to turn around fewer than 185 km (100 nautical miles) from their goal. The expeditioners' aim was to complete 'unfinished family business'.[17] Most of the focus, however, was on Amundsen and Scott. The BBC television documentary *Blizzard*, screened in 2006, staged a race with teams using replica clothes, equipment and food, in Greenland rather than the Antarctic in order to incorporate dogs; the Norwegians won. As the southern summer of 2011–12 approached, numerous teams began to converge on the Pole, many hoping to arrive in time for an official ceremony marking the 100th anniversary of Amundsen's first arrival, held on 14

High Latitude Antarctic Tourism: South Pole Inn, Anascaul, Ireland. Tom Crean, Antarctic expedition veteran and member of the support team for Scott's polar party, established this pub on his return to Ireland.

December 2011. Extreme World Races had begun organizing races at the South Pole in 2008–9 (the experience of the British team in the first event was filmed for the BBC documentary *On Thin Ice*), and held a Scott-Amundsen Centenary Race in 2011–12. Contestants left from the coast of Dronning Maud Land in East Antarctica, racing for first arrival at the Pole. The Norwegian team won. A more official Scott-Amundsen Centenary Race, launched by the Duke and Duchess of Cambridge, saw two teams – unassisted and unsupported – following the original routes, arriving in time for the official Scott centenary ceremony on 17 January 2012. Both teams were composed of British servicemen, raising money for The Royal British Legion. The 'Norwegians' won.

Not all centenary events were races; some were more concerned with honouring the details of the original events. Sørpolen 2011, a Norwegian expedition, aimed to replay Amundsen's daily progress, obviously without the aid of dogs. Logistical difficulties delayed the start, however, and two members had to be flown for the last 50 miles (80 km) in order to reach the Pole in time for the official centenary ceremony. They then skied north and retraced the last few miles to the Pole, joined by the Norwegian prime minister Jens Stoltenberg. The remaining two members duly arrived just before midnight, 'local' (New Zealand) time, having skied the entire way.[18] Another Norwegian expedition attempted a re-creation following the original route using replica dress and gear; the leader, Alse Johansen, also chose to be flown the last leg rather than miss the centenary. More than 100 visitors – as well as station personnel – were present for the official ceremony, which included the unveiling of a bust of Amundsen made from ice.[19]

The Scott centenary events were necessarily more subdued. A re-enactment of Scott's journey – or rather, a selected part of it – using period dress and equipment had been made a few years before the centenary in 2006, by a guided group raising money for charity. As they walked only the last 270 km (170 miles) of the journey, a stretch for which Scott's team relied solely on man-hauling, dogs and ponies were not required. The lighthearted aspects of sledging in Edwardian costume, however, would have been inappropriate for the actual centenary of a tragic journey. The ceremony marking the arrival of the British party was smaller than the Norwegian ceremony and – with its connotations of memorialization – more 'heartfelt', according to one observer.[20] In the summer of 2013–14, two British adventurers man-hauled Scott's original planned route to the Pole and back – the first to complete the journey. This was the longest distance covered by an unassisted polar expedition in history (although it was not technically unsupported, since they were forced to call in supplies at one point).

Many of the centenary expeditions and events were facilitated by Antarctic tourist companies. By the first decade of the twentieth century South Polar tourism was a well-established industry, catering to a steady niche market. Tourists had been coming to – or at least over – the Pole for decades. The earliest tourist flight occurred in 1968, when the Admiral Richard E. Byrd Polar Center, based in Boston, sponsored a flight over both poles, with 67 tourists on board. Pan American Airways made a similar bipolar overflight nine years later, to celebrate its 50th anniversary. These were one-off events, although the Magnetic South Pole near the East Antarctic coast saw a series of tourist overflights on Qantas aircraft in 1977, initiated by the Australian entrepreneur Dick Smith.[21] Commercial summer flights over the coastal areas

Four men recreate Scott's trek to the South Pole to raise money for cerebral palsy research.

Anne Noble's *Wilhelmina Bay, Antarctica* (2005) points ironically to the paradoxes of tourism in a place that is renowned for being 'untouched' by humans.

of the continent by Qantas and Air New Zealand became regular over the next few years, until the 1979 Mount Erebus disaster, in which all 247 occupants of an aircraft were killed when the plane they were in crashed into the mountain, put a stop to them for some time. Meanwhile, Antarctic cruise-ship tourism – continuously active since the late 1960s – had begun to burgeon. This was limited, obviously, to the coastal regions of the continent, mostly the spectacular and relatively accessible Antarctic Peninsula.

Tourism to the South Pole remained a much more difficult prospect. In order to fly economical numbers of tourists and cargo into the continent's interior, operators needed to use long-range aircraft with wheels (rather than skis), which can be flown intercontinentally from locations at the bottom of South America or South Africa. Given that just a tiny fraction of the Antarctic continent is exposed ground, and most of that is mountainous, ice runways were an obvious solution.[22] In the mid-1980s the

Ilyushin aircraft carrying Antarctic tourists approaches a blue-ice runway.

tour operator Adventure Network International (ANI) began looking for possible sites for a 'blue-ice' runway – usually found in the lee of mountain ranges, where wind scours the snow away and enables a wheeled landing. Settling on a place in the Patriot Hills, southwest of the Antarctic Peninsula at around 80 degrees latitude (roughly 1,000 km from the Pole), ANI began flying in paying customers in DC-4 aircraft in the summer of 1987–8. Some of these were mountaineers aiming to climb Antarctica's highest peak, Mount Vinson. Others had their eyes on the Pole, where they were flown by ski-equipped aircraft in early 1988 – the first tourists to do so. The following year the company offered its first guided journey to the South Pole, with a group of eleven people leaving from Hercules Inlet, on skis with support from snowmobiles. By 2005 ANI could boast of having 'supported virtually every expedition that has crossed the continent on foot, by vehicle or by aircraft'.[23] While there are other outfits offering trips to Antarctica's interior and to the Pole, ANI – since 2010 operating out of Union Glacier rather than the nearby Patriot Hills – has dominated South Polar tourism.

In the early twenty-first century if you are looking to travel to the South Pole, there is a range of options available to you, depending on your fitness level and motivation. You can find them easily, outlined in the chapter devoted to the South Pole in the Lonely Planet travel guide to Antarctica, or on a tourist operator's website. For the 'true adventurer', ANI offers traverses

Ilyushin aircraft deposits excited tourists on a blue-ice runway.

leaving from locations at the inward edge of the Ronne Ice Shelf. They cost around U.S.$65,000 (not including travel to and from Punta Arenas, Chile) and require months of training. For those looking for a 'serious challenge' but unable or unwilling to attempt this distance, there is the slightly cheaper option of 'Ski Last Degree', a distance of 111 km (60 nautical miles), which typically takes six days to cross. For 'polar enthusiasts', the option of camping at the South Pole overnight is available, at a site just 1 km away (half a mile) from Amundsen-Scott Station. ANI's

Mountaineers approaching Mount Vinson base camp (Vinson Massif behind).

promotional material here treads a line between maintaining a sense of intrepidness without the suggestion of privation. Prospective customers are offered 'a taste of polar exploration' as they 'camp overnight in an expedition-style tent', but are expected to be 'surprised how comfortable Antarctica can be!', with meals and recreation taking place in a heated tent. You can also fly from the ANI camp at Union Glacier to the Pole – a four- to five-hour flight – and return the same day; a tour of the scientific base is included.[24]

Given the extreme and remote conditions, South Polar tourism seems to have run remarkably smoothly, with one tragic exception. In 1997 a six-man private expedition travelled to the Pole to skydive, using an ANI chartered plane. A tandem pair – the first such jump at the South Pole – landed without incident; a third parachutist deployed his reserve chute only just in time to land safely. Three others did not deploy their parachutes at all and died upon impact. Considerable speculation has gone into the source of the tragedy. Befuddlement from hypoxia is one prominent possibility; the solo jumper who survived experienced

Approaching the South Pole via 150 km 'NGO access route'. Even at the Earth's southern extreme you need to follow a 'groomed path', to avoid entry into the Clean Air Sector or the Hazardous Zone associated with the buried original station.

'Ski Last Degree' tourists wave to their aircraft.

some confusion reading his altimeter on the way down. Although the skydivers jumped from around 2,400 m (8,000 ft) above the plateau, the Pole itself sits at 2,800 m (9,300 ft) above sea level. The thinner air through which the men jumped meant that the fall rate was significantly greater than it would have been had they jumped from 8,000 ft above sea level. The barometric pressure over the polar regions is slightly less than at lower latitudes, increasing the fall rate even more. The skydivers may not have mentally adjusted for the difference, particularly given that the blank white icescape would have provided few visual clues. Their deaths account for half of all fatalities at the Pole itself and had a significant impact upon the station's residents. As one remarked: 'Most people who have heard of this station don't think of it as someone's home – it's a station or a research facility or just a tourist attraction. But we were home, and our home had been hit by tragedy.'[25]

Antarctic tourism raises considerable concerns, not only for reasons of safety, but environmental impact. In the early 1990s the International Association of Antarctic Tour Operators was

Tourists travelling to the Pole by ski must carry all their own food, as well as rubbish and human waste.

formed in order to specify guidelines for tourism in the region. ANI was a founding member, and prides itself on its environmental credentials: unlike Amundsen-Scott South Pole Station, the company flies its human waste out of the continent for disposal, and dismantles its camp at the Pole at the end of every summer.[26] One of the greatest concerns about Antarctic tourism – the massive growth in numbers since the 1990s – has less relevance to the South Pole. Total Antarctic tourist numbers peaked at around 46,000 in the summer of 2007–8, and although they dipped with the global financial crisis that occurred around this time, they remain in the tens of thousands. The vast majority of these tourists travel to the continent's coastal areas on cruise ships; only around 100 of them annually visit the South Pole by various means and operators.[27] Although in the early 1990s one of the pioneers of blue-ice runways raised the spectacle of a Boeing 747 disgorging hundreds of tourists onto the ice, the high cost of polar tourism – even a South Pole overnight stay costs around U.S.$50,000 – has kept numbers steadily low.[28]

The gift shop at the end of the Earth.

This exclusivity is in itself key to the success of South Polar tourism: mass numbers would detract considerably from the sense of isolation and adventure that still draws people to the place. The comparatively small number of visitors gives something of the sense of 'firstness' that attracts South Polar travellers: those on the first tourist flight paid an extra $10,000 to land a quarter of an hour ahead of the next.[29] In the second decade of the twenty-first century tour operators still present arrival at the Pole as 'a feat that very few people have achieved'.[30] One researcher notes that, even among cruise-ship travellers, the word 'tourist' is avoided. Instead, the journey is an 'expedition':

> tourists are regarded and treated as expeditioners, people who are not merely sightseers but intrepid travellers venturing into the pristine icy waters and the unexplored continent beyond . . . To experience travel that is uncomfortable, risky and potentially dangerous is to give people the legitimate right to place themselves appropriately within the hierarchy of travellers.[31]

Danger, risk and discomfort are relative, however. In his description of life at the Pole, Nicholas Johnson recalls seeing a group of people at the station bar who had skied the 'Last Degree'. 'So they paid to ski across a piece of map?', he asks a local. 'You got it', she replies, 'Then they get a free cup of coffee, a hero shot at the Pole, and a boot in the ass to get out.' Johnson notes that 'While tourists on plane flights are generally either ignored or treated to hair-trigger courtesy, Polies are more enthusiastic about cross-continent expeditioners who actually work for their glory.'[32] Amundsen-Scott Station caters, nonetheless, to non-heroic tourists, offering a visitors' centre and gift shop where they can buy mementos of their journey.

And even for those who traverse, there are degrees of achievement. Some authorities, such as Headland, do not recognize the ANI journeys that leave from Hercules Inlet or the 'Messner Start' as full traverses; while ANI considers these departure points to be at the edge of the continent, they are at the inward end of a large ice shelf, which for Headland is 'well inland'.[33] Then there is the distinction between independent adventurers, who almost always use ANI for logistical support, and those who pay to be guided across the continent. A good example can be found in an account by Joseph Murphy of the earliest guided expedition, which included Murden and Metz, the first women to reach the Pole – presuming, that is, that their traverse, which left from the inward edge of the Ronne Ice Shelf, 'counts'. According to Murphy, the two women became agitated upon hearing their upcoming experience described as a 'tour': 'I'm not going to spend $70,000 for a tourist trip . . . I thought it was an expedition – not a *tour*! . . . If it's just a commercial tour, I don't want to go!'[34] In her book

To the Poles without a Beard, Hartley is also acutely aware of expedition hierarchies, reporting her sense of rejection when she overhears her guide remarking that an independent women's team behind them deserves the real glory. 'I was on a "commercial" expedition, if you like', Hartley reflects, 'I was paying to be guided to the Pole'. Yet, while 'pathologically against' being referred to as an 'explorer' and preferring the term 'extreme tourist', Hartley maintains the significance of her traverse as a 'personal journey'.[35]

From a number of perspectives, the concept of South Polar tourism is absurd. Apart from the scientific station and a collection of markers, there is little to see. Being able to buy a souvenir in the gift shop is a mixed blessing – although it might have a certain kitsch cachet, it brings the sublime and the ridiculous a little too close together, reminding you that you are, indeed, a tourist. The two defunct polar stations, which might give a sense of heritage, are now gone. Unless your journey has been arduous and impressive, the locals may well be dismissive of what, for you, is a significant personal experience. You can be confident of your operator's environmental credentials in this famously pristine icescape, but your carbon footprint in travelling so far from home is not insignificant. Surrounding you is a white plateau, stretching in all directions; there are no natural sites to attract the eye, or to which you might make a short excursion. The temperatures make being outdoors for very long a trial. Experiencing cold that intense is of course noteworthy in itself – but then, the average temperatures of a South Pole summer (the only season accessible to tourists) could be experienced in winter in parts of Russia or Canada for far less money.

Despite all this, the South Pole retains its allure as a travel destination. In the early twenty-first century, it seems, it still means something to stand at the Earth's axis, to get off the turning planet for just a night, or even an hour; to be simultaneously on the map's edge and at the world's centre.

Skiing to the
South Pole.

CHRONOLOGY

1773	A voyage led by British naval captain James Cook makes an inaugural crossing of the Antarctic circle
1774	Cook's expedition achieves a farthest south of 71°10′
1820	Three reported sightings of the Antarctic continent: by a Russian exploratory expedition led by Thaddeus Bellingshausen; a British naval voyage led by Edward Bransfield; and an American sealing voyage led by Nathaniel B. Palmer
1821	American sealing captain John Davis makes what is probably the first landing on the continent
1823	British sealing captain James Weddell achieves a new farthest south of 74°15′
1841	James Clark Ross, leading a British naval expedition, locates the position of the Magnetic South Pole
1842	Ross's expedition achieves new farthest south of 78°10′
1899	Norwegian-born Carsten Borchgrevink leads the first expedition to spend a winter on the Antarctic continent, makes a brief overland journey and betters Ross's farthest south by a small margin
1902	A three-man party led by Robert F. Scott makes the first substantial sledging journey towards the South Pole, achieving a farthest south of 82°17′
1909	A four-man party led by Ernest Shackleton comes within 100 nautical miles of the South Pole, achieving a farthest south of 88°23′
1909	Three members of Shackleton's expedition reach the vicinity of the Magnetic South Pole
1911	A five-man Norwegian team led by Roald Amundsen reaches the South Pole on 14 December
1912	A five-man team led by Scott also reaches the Pole, on 17 January; all members die on the return journey

1929 An American expedition led by naval aviator Richard E. Byrd makes first flight over the Pole
1956 A U.S. Navy aircraft lands at the South Pole; Rear Admiral George J. Dufek and companions become first people to set foot at the South Pole since Scott's men
1957 First station at the South Pole begins operation
1957–8 International Geophysical Year: as part of this coordinated scientific effort, twelve nations establish over 50 stations in the Antarctic.
1958 New Zealander Edmund Hillary, as part of the Commonwealth Trans-Antarctic Expedition, leads tractor journey to the South Pole – the first overland traverse since Scott
1959 Antarctic Treaty signed (enters into force in 1961)
1965 First flight over the South Pole by a private plane, *The Pole Cat*
1968 First tourist flight over the South Pole
1969 First time women stand at the South Pole
1970 First civilian flight arrives at the South Pole
1975 New National Science Foundation 'Dome' Station at the South Pole begins operation
1988 First tourist flight arrives at the South Pole
1989 First guided tourist traversing group arrives at the South Pole
1991 Madrid Protocol signed (enters into force in 1998)
1993 Norwegian Erling Kagge makes first unassisted, unsupported solo journey to the Pole
2002–6 Construction of 'South Pole Traverse' – compacted snow route between McMurdo and the Pole
2008 Third South Pole station officially opened
2011–12 Amundsen/Scott centenary expeditions and ceremonies
2048 Madrid Protocol prohibiting mining in Antarctica will be open for review

REFERENCES

1 Where is the South Pole?

1 Roald Amundsen, *The South Pole: An Account of the Norwegian Antarctic Expedition in the 'Fram', 1910–1912* (London, 2001), vol. II, p. 121.
2 Ibid, pp. 132–3.
3 Robert Falcon Scott, *Journals: Captain Scott's Last Expedition*, ed. Max Jones (Oxford, 2006), 18 January 1912, p. 377.
4 Olav Orheim, 'The Present Location of the Tent that Roald Amundsen Left Behind at the South Pole in December 1911', *Polar Record*, XLVII (2011), p. 269.
5 Peter Rejcek, 'A Good Point', *Antarctic Sun*, 1 January 2010, available at http://antarcticsun.usap.gov.
6 Jeremy D. Stilwell and John A. Long, *Frozen in Time: Prehistoric Life in Antarctica* (Collingwood, Vic, 2011), pp. 13–15.
7 J. L. Chen et al., 'Rapid Ice Melting Drives Earth's Pole to the East', *Geophysical Research Letters*, XL/11 (16 June 2013), pp. 2625–30.
8 The empirical data available for the North Pole is missing for its more remote cousin. See Giancarlo Scalera, 'TPW and Polar Motion as Due to an Asymmetrical Earth Expansion', *Annals of Geophysics*, Supplement to XLIX/1 (2006), pp. 496–7.
9 Chen et al., 'Rapid Ice'.
10 Aristotle, *On the Heavens*, 285b8ff; *Meteorologica*, 362a32ff.
11 This summary of ancient Greek and medieval conceptions of the South Pole is drawn from Dirk L. Couprie, *Heaven and Earth in Ancient Greek Cosmology: From Thales to Heraclides Ponticus* (New York and London, 2011), and personal communication (email, 17 April 2013).
12 Gillian Turner, *North Pole, South Pole: The Epic Quest to Solve the Great Mystery of Earth's Magnetism* (New York, 2011), pp. 9, 14–17, 23.
13 Ibid., pp. 23, 34–44.

14 Ibid., pp. 53–4.
15 James Ross, in John Ross, *Narrative of a Second Voyage in Search of a North-west Passage, and of a Residence in the Arctic Regions during the Years 1829, 1830, 1831, 1832, 1833: Including the Reports of Commander, now Captain, James Clark Ross* (London, 1835), p. 558.
16 Coordinates for the magnetic poles at five-year intervals from 1900 to 2015 can be found at 'Magnetic Poles', British Geological Survey, available at www.geomag.bgs.ac.uk.
17 Nicola Jones, 'Tracking the Magnetic South Pole', *Nature News*, 28 December 2011, available at www.nature.com.
18 Letter to Arthur Swindells, 17 November 1911, Andrew Inglis Clark papers C4/M90. Rare and Special Collections, University of Tasmania Library.
19 See Bernadette Hince, *The Antarctic Dictionary: A Complete Guide to Antarctic English* (Collingwood, Vic, 2000), p. 338.
20 T. S. Eliot, 'Burnt Norton' in *Four Quartets*, in *Collected Poems, 1909–1962* (London and Boston, MA, 1974), p. 191.

2 Maps and Mythologies

1 Bernadette Hince, 'Something's Missing Down There', programme transcript, *Ockham's Razor*, Radio National, 10 October 2004, available at www.abc.net.au.
2 Aristotle, *On the Heavens*, 285b8ff, and *Meteorologica*, 362a32ff.
3 Gillian Turner, *North Pole, South Pole: The Epic Quest to Solve the Great Mystery of Earth's Magnetism* (New York, 2011), p. 10.
4 Nathaniel Harris, *Mapping the World: Maps and their History* (London, 2002), p. 62.
5 Jorge Guzmán-Gutiérrez, 'Imaging and Mapping Antarctica and the Southern Ocean', *Imago Mundi*, LXII/2 (2010), p. 264.
6 Robert Clancy, *The Mapping of Terra Australis* (Macquarie Park, NSW, 1995), p. 122.
7 Gregory C. McIntosh, *The Piri Reis Map of 1513* (Athens, GA, and London, 2000), p. 63.
8 Corneille Wytfliet, 'Chica sive Patagonica et Avstralis Terra' from *Histoire universelle des Indes occidentales et orientales* (1597). The map can be viewed online at the State Library of New South Wales 'Finding Antarctica' exhibition website – see 'Associations and Websites' at the end of this book.
9 Andrew Gosling, 'Unexpected Treasures from Asia', *National Library Magazine* [Australia] (June 2011), p. 5.
10 Chet Van Duzer, 'Cartographic Invention: The Southern Continent on Vatican MS Urb. Lat. 274, Folios 73v–74r (*c.* 1530)', *Imago Mundi*, XXIX/2 (2007), p. 202.

11 Christopher Wortham, 'Meanings of the South: From the *Mappaemundi* to Shakespeare's *Othello*', in *European Perceptions of 'Terra Australis'*, ed. Anne Scott et al. (Farnham, Surrey, and Burlington, VT, 2011), p. 65; Dirk L. Courpie, personal communication (email, 20 June 2013).
12 Sanjay Chaturvedi, *Dawning of Antarctica: A Geopolitical Analysis* (New Delhi, 1990), p. 17.
13 McIntosh, *The Piri Reis Map*, chapter 6.
14 Roslynn D. Haynes, 'Astronomy and the Dreaming: The Astronomy of the Aboriginal Australians', *Astronomy Across Cultures: The History of Non-Western Astronomy*, ed. Helaine Selin (Boston, MA, and London, 2000) p. 59; and personal communication (email, 18 April 2013).
15 Johannes Wilbert, ed., *Folk Literature of the Selknam Indians: Martin Gusinde's Collection of Selknam Narratives* (Los Angeles, CA, 1975), p. 141.
16 Turi McFarlane, 'Maori Associations with the Antarctic / Tiro o te Moana ki re Tonga', Graduate Certificate in Antarctic Studies thesis, University of Canterbury, Christchurch (2007), p. 5, available at www.anta.canterbury.ac.nz.
17 Chet Van Duzer, 'The Mythic Geography of the Northern Polar Regions: *Inventio fortunata* and Buddhist Cosmology', *Culturas Populares: Revista Electrónica*, II (2006), p. 8; Rodney W. Shirley, *The Mapping of the New World: Early Printed World Maps, 1472–1700* (London, 1987), p. 26.
18 Van Duzer, 'Mythic Geography', p. 9.
19 Chet Van Duzer, 'The Cartography, Geography, and Hydrography of the Southern Ring Continent, 1515–1763', *Orbis Terrarum*, VIII (2002), p. 137.
20 James Ross, in John Ross, *Narrative of a Second Voyage in Search of a North-west Passage, and of a Residence in the Arctic Regions during the Years 1829, 1830, 1831, 1832, 1833: Including the Reports of Commander, now Captain, James Clark Ross* (London, 1835), p. 555.
21 Quoted in Bill Leadbetter, 'The Roman South', in *European Perceptions of 'Terra Australis'*, p. 47.
22 Joseph E. Schwartzberg, 'An Eighteenth-century Cosmographic Globe from India', *Cartographica*, XXX (1993), p. 83.
23 Ibid., p. 75; Chaturvedi, *Dawning of Antarctica*, p. 17.
24 Joscelyn Godwin, *Arktos: The Polar Myth in Science, Symbolism and Nazi Survival* (Kempton, IL, 1996), pp. 125, 134.
25 Victoria Nelson, *The Secret Life of Puppets* (Cambridge, MA, 2001), pp. 139, 145, 148.
26 Carpenter's film is based on the novella 'Who Goes There?' (1938) by John W. Campbell Jr, set at the Magnetic South Pole.

27 It seems to have derived from a letter Shackleton wrote to a friend in 1917, in which he referred to 'my own White South'. See Margery Fisher and James Fisher, *Shackleton* (London, 1957), p. 330.
28 Ranulph Fiennes, 'Introduction: This Endless Horizon', in Kari Herbert and Huw Lewis-Jones, *In Search of the South Pole* (London, 2011), p. 17.
29 Quoted in Herbert and Lewis-Jones, *In Search of the South Pole*, p. 168.
30 Thomas Pynchon, *V* (Philadelphia, PA, and New York, 1963), pp. 241, 204–6.
31 Elena Glasberg, *Antarctica as Cultural Critique: The Gendered Politics of Scientific Exploration and Climate Change* (New York, 2012), p. 9.
32 Laura Kurgan, *Close Up at a Distance: Mapping, Technology, and Politics* (New York, 2013), p. 9.
33 Ben Cosgrove, 'Home, Sweet Home: In Praise of the "Blue Marble"', *life.com*, available at http://life.time.com, accessed 15 April 2015.

3 Polar Imaginations

1 Jules Verne, *Twenty Thousand Leagues Under the Seas*, trans. William Butcher (Oxford, 1998), p. 312.
2 Dante Alighieri, *The Divine Comedy*, trans. H. R. Huse (San Francisco, CA, 1954), *Inferno*, Canto 26, lines 127–8.
3 *Relation d'un voyage du Pole Arctique, au Pole Antarctique, par le centre du monde . . .* (Amsterdam, 1721). Quotations are from translated excerpts in *Subterranean Worlds: A Critical Anthology*, ed. Peter Fitting (Middletown, CT, 2004), pp. 27–8.
4 A common assumption about the South Polar regions in early fiction was that they were shrouded in continual darkness. See Fitting, ed., *Subterranean Worlds*, p. 199.
5 Joseph Hall, *Another World and Yet the Same: Bishop Joseph Hall's 'Mundus alter et idem'* (New Haven, CT, 1981), pp. 79–84.
6 Daniel Defoe, *A New Voyage Round the World, by a Course Never Sailed Before* (London, 1725 [1724]), p. 189.
7 Christopher Spotswood, *Voyage of Will Rogers to the South Pole* (Launceston, Tasmania, 1888), p. 30.
8 George McIver, *Neuroomia: A New Continent. A Manuscript Delivered from the Deep* (London, Melbourne, Sydney, Adelaide and Brisbane, 1894), p. 136.
9 W. E. Johns, *Biggles Breaks the Silence* (London, 1949), p. 31.
10 Quoted in David Fausett, *Images of the Antipodes in the Eighteenth Century: A Study in Stereotyping* (Amsterdam, 1995), p. 155.

11 James De Mille, *A Strange Manuscript Found in a Copper Cylinder* (Ottawa, 1986), pp. 179–80.
12 Frank Cowan, *Revi-Lona: A Romance of Love in a Marvellous Land* (New York, 1978), p. 3.
13 Ibid., *Revi-Lona*, p. 68.
14 Edgar Allan Poe, 'MS Found in a Bottle', in *Selected Tales* (Oxford and New York, 1980), pp. 15–16.
15 Edgar Allan Poe, *The Narrative of Arthur Gordon Pym of Nantucket* (New York, 1999), pp. 216–17.
16 James Fenimore Cooper, *The Monikins* [1835] (Albany, NY, 1990), p. 117.
17 Thomas Erskine, *Armata* [1817], in *Modern British Utopias*, ed. Gregory Claeys (London, 1997), vol. VI, p. 7.

4 Pole-hunting

1 W. B. Maxwell, *Spinster of this Parish* (New York, 1922), pp. 116–17.
2 John Watson Cummins, 'Himself and Mr Maxwell: The Life and Works of W. B. Maxwell (1866–1938)', PhD thesis, University of Pennsylvania (1964), p. 164.
3 Roald Amundsen, *The South Pole: An Account of the Norwegian Antarctic Expedition in the 'Fram', 1910–1912*, trans. A. G. Chater [1912] (London, 2002), vol. I, p. 3.
4 Ibid.
5 James Cook, *A Voyage Towards the South Pole, and Round the World* (Adelaide, 1970), vol. I, pp. xvii, 3, 267–8.
6 James Weddell, *A Voyage Towards the South Pole Performed in the Years 1822–24, Containing an Examination of the Antarctic Sea* (Newton Abbot, Devon, 1970), pp. 37, 281.
7 Jules S.-C. Dumont d'Urville, *Two Voyages to the South Seas*, trans. Helen Rosenman (Collingwood, Vic, 1987), vol. II, p. 318.
8 Granville Allen Mawer, *South by Northwest: The Magnetic Crusade and the Contest for Antarctica* (Kent Town, SA, 2006), p. 28.
9 Charles Wilkes, *Narrative of the United States Exploring Expedition. During the Years 1838, 1839, 1840, 1841, 1842* (London, 1845), vol. I, p. xxvi.
10 James Clark Ross, *A Voyage of Discovery and Research in the Southern and Antarctic Regions During the Years 1839–43* (Cambridge, 2011), vol. I, p. xxiv.
11 Ibid., p. 246.
12 H. J. Bull, *The Cruise of the 'Antarctic' to the South Polar Regions* (London and New York, 1896), p. 233.

13 Carsten Borchgrevink, *First on the Antarctic Continent: Being an Account of the British Antarctic Expedition, 1898–1900* (London and Canberra, 1980), p. 1.
14 Michael H. Rosove, *Let Heroes Speak: Antarctic Explorers, 1772–1922* (New York, 2002), p. 76.
15 Mawer, *South by Northwest*, p. 165.
16 William S. Bruce, quoted in Innes M. Keighren, 'Of Poles, Pressmen and the Newspaper Public: Reporting the Scottish National Antarctic Expedition, 1902-1904', *Scottish Geographical Journal*, CXXI/2 (2005), p. 211.
17 Robert F. Scott, *The Voyage of the 'Discovery'*, vol. I (Stroud, 2005), p. 32.
18 Clements Markham, *Lands of Silence: A History of Arctic and Antarctic Exploration* (Cambridge, 1912), p. 453.
19 Edward Wilson, *Diary of the 'Discovery' Expedition to the Antarctic, 1901–1904* (London, 1966), 12 June 1902, p. 151.
20 Scott, *Voyage of the 'Discovery'*, vol. II, p. 71.
21 Edgeworth David, in E. H. Shackleton, *The Heart of the Antarctic: Being the Story of the British Antarctic Expedition, 1907–1909* (Philadelphia, PA, 1909), vol. II, p. 179.
22 M. E. David, *Professor David: The Life of Edgeworth David* (London, 1937), pp. 164–5.
23 Edgeworth David, in Shackleton, *Heart of the Antarctic*, vol. II, p. 181.
24 Douglas Mawson, *Mawson's Antarctic Diaries*, ed. Fred Jacka and Eleanor Jacka (Crows Nest, NSW, 2008), p. 46.
25 Philip Ayres, *Mawson: A Life* (Carlton, Vic, 1999), p. 70.
26 Quoted in Margery Fisher and James Fisher, *Shackleton* (London, 1957), p. 219.
27 Amundsen, *South Pole*, vol. I, p. 42; vol. II, p. 121.
28 Ibid., vol. I, p. 45.
29 Ibid., p. 52.
30 Ibid., vol. II, p. 133.
31 Shirase Antarctic Expedition Supporters' Association, *The Japanese South Polar Expedition, 1910–12*, trans. Lara Dagnell and Hilary Shibata (Norwich and Huntingdon, 2011), p. 88.
32 'Shirase', Scott Polar Research Institute website, available at www.spri.cam.ac.uk, accessed 15 April 2015.
33 Robert Falcon Scott, *Journals: Scott's Last Expedition* (Oxford, 2006), 17 January 1912, p. 376.
34 Ibid., 16 January 1912, p. 376.
35 Ibid., October 1911, p. 302.
36 Theodore K. Mason, *The South Pole Ponies: The Forgotten Heroes of Antarctic Exploration* (Glasgow, KY, 2007), p. 94.
37 Scott, *Journals*, 3 January 1912, p. 365.

38 Ibid., 17 January 1912, p. 376; and ibid., 18 January 1912, p. 377.
39 Ibid., 19 January 1912, p. 380.
40 Ibid., 7 February 1912, p. 391.
41 Ibid., 16 February 1912, p. 396.
42 Ibid., 19 February 1912, p. 399.
43 Ibid., 6 March 1912, p. 407.
44 Ibid., 16 or 17 March 1912, p. 410.
45 Ibid., 29 March 1912, p. 412.
46 Amundsen, *South Pole*, vol. I, pp. 237–8.
47 Simon Nasht, *The Last Explorer: Hubert Wilkins, Australia's Unknown Hero* (Sydney, 2005), pp. 177–8.
48 Quoted in David Burke, *Moments of Terror: The Story of Antarctic Aviation* (Kensington, NSW, 1994), p. 53.
49 Richard E. Byrd, *Little America: Aerial Exploration in the Antarctic and the Flight to the South Pole* (London, 1931), p. 240.
50 Edmund Hillary, *View from the Summit: The Remarkable Memoir by the First Person to Conquer Everest* (New York, 2000), p. 180.

5 Settling in at 'Ninety South'

1 Quoted in Paul Siple, *90° South: The Story of the American South Pole Conquest* (New York, 1959), p. 20.
2 Kim Stanley Robinson, *Antarctica* [1997] (London, 1998), pp. 224, 227.
3 Jerri Nielsen, with Maryanne Vollers, *Ice Bound: One Woman's Incredible Battle for Survival at the South Pole* (London, 2001), p. 67.
4 William L. Fox, *Terra Incognita: Looking into the Emptiest Continent* (San Antonio, TX, 2005), p. 107.
5 Nicholas Johnson, *Big Dead Place: Inside the Strange and Menacing World of Antarctica* (Los Angeles, CA, 2005), p. 90.
6 Siple, *90° South*, p. 170.
7 Ibid., p. 228.
8 Ibid., p. 176.
9 Paul Siple, 'We are Living at the South Pole', *National Geographic Magazine*, CXII/1 (1957), p. 14.
10 Ibid., p. 20.
11 Siple, *90° South*, pp. 238, 219, 221, 270–71; 'We are Living at the South Pole', p. 29.
12 Siple, *90° South*, pp. 205, 263, 268–74.
13 Ibid., pp. 208–9.
14 Ibid., p. 340.
15 National Science Foundation (NSF), 'U.S. South Pole Station: Celebrating a Century of Science and Exploration', accessible at www.nsf.gov, accessed 15 April 2015.

16 Nielsen, *Ice Bound*, p. 47.
17 NSF, 'U.S. South Pole Station'.
18 Nielsen, *Ice Bound*, pp. 47–8.
19 Ibid., p. 52.
20 Connie Samaras, 'American Dreams', *Scholar and Feminist Online*, VII/1 (Fall 2008), available at http://sfonline.barnard.edu, p. 4.
21 Robinson, *Antarctica*, pp. 222, 227. Robinson visited the Pole in 1995 with the NSF Artists and Writers Program and his novel *Antarctica* was published the same year that Congress approved the construction of the new station.
22 Siple, *90° South*, pp. 322, 308–9, 317–18.
23 Elizabeth Chipman, *Women on the Ice: A History of Women in the Far South* (Carlton, Vic, 1986), p. 101.
24 Bill Spindler, 'Winterover Statistics', available at www.southpolestation.com, accessed 15 April 2015.
25 Samaras, 'American Dreams', p. 5.
26 Mark Andrew Cravalho, 'Toast on Ice: The Ethnopsychology of the Winter-over Experience in Antarctica', *Ethos*, XXIV (1996), pp. 628–56.
27 Johnson, *Big Dead Place*, p. 92.
28 Spindler, 'Winterover Statistics'.
29 Nielsen, *Ice Bound*, pp. 58–9.
30 Siple, *90° South*, pp. 307, 248, 310–11.
31 Nielsen, *Ice Bound*, p. 28.
32 K. T. Natani and J. T. Shurley, 'Sociopsychological Aspects of a Winter Vigil at South Pole Station', *Antarctic Research Series*, XXII (1974), p. 89.
33 Lawrence A. Palinkas, 'The Psychology of Isolated and Confined Environments: Understanding Human Behavior in Antarctica', *American Psychologist*, LVIII/5 (May 2003), p. 358.
34 Siple, 'We are Living at the South Pole', p. 23; *90° South*, pp. 308–9.
35 Nielsen, *Ice Bound*, p. 51.
36 Douglas Mawson, *The Home of the Blizzard* (London, 1915), vol. I, p. 146.
37 Siple, *90° South*, pp. 274–5, 315.
38 Bill Spindler, 'A South Pole Wedding', available at www.southpolestation.com, 15 June 2011.

6 Highest, Coldest, Driest . . . ?

1 Valérie Masson-Delmotte, 'Ice with Everything', in *Antarctica: Global Science from a Frozen Continent*, ed. David W. H. Walton (Cambridge, 2013), p. 99.

2 Bryan Storey, 'A Keystone in a Changing World', in *Antarctica: Global Science from a Frozen Continent*, p. 38.

3 Matthew A. Lazzara et al., 'Fifty-year Amundsen–Scott South Pole Station Surface Climatology', *Atmospheric Research*, CXVIII (2012), p. 245.

4 John J. Cassano, 'Climate of Extremes', in *Antarctica: Global Science from a Frozen Continent*, p. 120.

5 Masson-Delmotte, 'Ice with Everything', p. 78; 'Antarctic Specially Managed Area No. 5: Amundsen-Scott South Pole Station, South Pole: Climate', available at http://www.southpole.aq.

6 XiangBin Cui et al., 'Ice Radar Investigation at Dome A, East Antarctica: Ice Thickness and Subglacial Topography', *Chinese Science Bulletin*, LV/4–5 (2010), p. 425.

7 Masson-Delmotte, 'Ice with Everything', p. 73.

8 University of Wisconsin-Madison, IceCube, 'Antarctic Weather', available at http://icecube.wisc.edu/pole/weather.

9 Lazzara et al., 'Fifty-year Amundsen-Scott South Pole Station Surface Climatology', p. 249.

10 Paul Siple, 'We are Living at the South Pole', *National Geographic Magazine*, CXII/1 (1957), p. 23.

11 Paul Siple, *90° South: The Story of the American South Pole Conquest* (New York, 1959), p. 316.

12 Robert Falcon Scott, *Journals: Captain Scott's Last Expedition* (Oxford, 2006), 22 June 1911, p. 233.

13 Walter Tape, *Atmospheric Halos*, Antarctic Research Series, LXIV (Washington, DC, 1994), p. 1.

14 Ibid.

15 Scott, *Journals*, 13 May 1911, p. 191.

16 Glen E. Liston, 'Green Flash Observations on 24/25 March 1983 at the South Pole, Antarctica', *Weather*, LVI (January 2001), pp. 2–3.

17 Scott, *Journals*, 2 January 1912, p. 365.

18 B. Axelrod, 'Observations of South Polar Skuas at Dome C', *Antarctic Journal of the U.S.*, XIV/5 (1979), p. 173.

19 Arthur B. Ford, 'Skua and Petrel Sightings in the Interior Antarctic Ranges: Thiel and Southern Pensacola Mountains', *Antarctic Journal of the U.S.*, XVIII/5 (1983), p. 219.

20 Peter Convey, Angelika Brandt and Steve Nicol, 'Life in a Cold Environment', in *Antarctica: Global Science from a Frozen Continent*, pp. 194–5.

21 Ibid., p. 196.

22 R. D. Seppelt, 'Phytogeography of Continental Antarctic Lichens', *Lichenologist*, XXVII/6 (1995), p. 420.

23 Nicholas Johnson, *Big Dead Place: Inside the Strange and Menacing World of Antarctica* (Los Angeles, CA, 2005), p. 82.

24 Roald Amundsen, *The South Pole: An Account of the Norwegian Antarctic Expedition in the 'Fram', 1910–1912*, trans. A. G. Chater (London, 1912), vol. II, p. 122.
25 Siple, *90° South*, p. 178.
26 Bill Spindler, 'The Pole Pet Puppy Debacle', available at http://www.southpolestation.com, accessed 22 April 2015.
27 Most of this summary of introduced animals in Antarctica is based on R. K. Headland, 'History of Exotic Terrestrial Mammals in Antarctic Regions', *Polar Record*, XLVIII (2012), pp. 138–40.
28 Storey, 'A Keystone in a Changing World', pp. 48–51.
29 Ibid., pp. 56, 63–5.
30 Jeffrey D. Stilwell and John A. Long, *Frozen in Time: Prehistoric Life in Antarctica* (Collingwood, Vic, 2011), p. 185.
31 Storey, 'Antarctica', p. 48.
32 Written by Peter Van Dresser, the tale appeared in *Amazing Stories*, V/5 (August 1930), pp. 416–27, 468.
33 G. D. Trigg, 'Negotiation of a Minerals Regime', in *The Antarctic Treaty Regime: Law, Environment and Resources*, ed. G. D. Trigg (Cambridge, 1987), p. 182.
34 Ibid.
35 Olav Orheim, 'Managing the Frozen Commons', in *Antarctica: Global Science from a Frozen Continent*, pp. 286–7.
36 Masson-Delmotte, 'Ice with Everything', p. 92.
37 Ibid., p. 98; Alan Rodger, 'Antarctica: A Global Change Perspective', in *Antarctica: Global Science from a Frozen Continent*, p. 305.
38 Rodger, 'Antarctica: A Global Change Perspective', p. 306.
39 Ibid.
40 Jonathan Amos, 'Antarctic Ice Volume Measured', *BBC News: Science and Environment*, 8 March 2013, available at www.bbc.co.uk/news. The report of the original research project, Bedmap2, can be found at www.antarctica.ac.uk.
41 Masson-Delmotte, 'Ice with Everything', p. 92.
42 J. L. Chen et al., 'Rapid Ice Melting Drives Earth's Pole to the East', *Geophysical Research Letters* (accepted manuscript online), 13 May 2013, DOI: 10.1002/grl.50552, available at http://onlinelibrary.wiley.com.

7 Looking Up and Looking Down

1 Michael G. Burton, 'Astronomy in Antarctica', *Astronomy and Astrophysics Review*, XVIII (2010), p. 417. 'Best seeing' refers to a minimum atmospheric blurring of the image.

2 Steve Martaindale, 'Pole an Ideal Spot for Astronomers', *Antarctic Sun*, 21 January 2007, available at antarcticsun.usap.gov.
3 Ibid.
4 Burton, 'Astronomy in Antarctica', pp. 431, 436–7, 439.
5 Will Saunders et al., 'Where is the Best Site on Earth? Domes A, B, C and F, and Ridges A and B', *Publications of the Astronomical Society of the Pacific*, CXXI (2009), pp. 976–92.
6 Burton, 'Astronomy in Antarctica', p. 420.
7 Ibid., p. 440.
8 'BICEP Flexes its Muscles', *The Economist* (22 March 2014), pp. 78–9.
9 Statistics provided here are drawn from 'IceCube Quick Facts', University of Wisconsin-Madison, available at icecube.wisc.edu, accessed 22 April 2015.
10 U.S. Geological Survey (USGS), 'Science Picks – USGS Seismology at the South Pole', available at www.usgs.gov, accessed 22 April 2015.
11 Ibid.
12 Gabrielle Walker, *Antarctica: An Intimate Portrait of the World's Most Mysterious Continent* (London, 2012), p. 198.
13 South Pole ASMA, 'Seismology', available via http://www.southpole.aq; USGS, 'Seismology at the South Pole'.
14 Jean Robert Petit, 'The Vostok Venture: An Outcome of the Antarctic Treaty', in *Science Diplomacy: Antarctica, Science, and the Governance of International Spaces*, ed. Paul Berkman et al. (Washington, DC, 2011), p. 167.
15 P. B. Price, K. Woschnagg and D. Chirkin, 'Age *vs* Depth of Glacial Ice at South Pole', *Geophysical Research Letters*, XXVII/14 (15 July 2000), pp. 2129–32.
16 Peter Rejcek, 'SPICE-ing It Up', *Antarctic Sun*, 8 March 2013, available at antarcticsun.usap.gov.
17 Ibid.
18 B.W. Davis, 'Science and Politics in Antarctic and Southern Oceans Policy: A Critical Assessment', in *Antarctica's Future: Continuity or Change?*, ed. R. A. Herr, H. R. Hall and M. G. Haward (Hobart, 1990), p. 39.

8 South Polar Politics

1 Ariel Dorfman, *The Nanny and the Iceberg* [1999] (New York, 2003), p. 56.
2 Paul Siple, *90° South: The Story of the American South Pole Conquest* (New York, 1959), pp. 16, 77, 360.
3 For Amundsen, see Roald Amundsen, *The South Pole: An Account of the Norwegian Antarctic Expedition in the 'Fram', 1910–12*, trans.

A. G. Chater [1912] (London, 2002), vol. II, p. 122; for Scott see Max Jones, *The Last Great Quest: Captain Scott's Antarctic Sacrifice* (Oxford, 2003), p. 74.
4 Hilary Shibata, 'Lt Shirase and the Japanese Antarctic Expedition of 1910–12: The Historical Background', *The Japanese South Polar Expedition 1910–12*, by the Shirase Antarctic Expedition Supporters' Association, trans. Lara Dagnell and Hilary Shibata (Norwich and Huntingdon, 2011), p. 15.
5 Ibid., p. 173.
6 The history of territorial claims is outlined in a number of publications. This summary is particularly indebted to Peter Beck, *The International Politics of Antarctica* (London, 1986), pp. 21–45 and 119–22; Christopher C. Joyner, *Governing the Frozen Commons: The Antarctic Regime and Environmental Protection* (Columbia, SC, 1988), pp. 14–20; and Klaus Dodds, *The Antarctic: A Very Short Introduction* (Oxford, 2012), pp. 48–68.
7 Victor Prescott and Gillian Triggs, *International Frontiers and Boundaries: Law, Politics and Geography* (Leiden, 2008), pp. 375–8.
8 Jan-Gunnar Winther et al., *Norway in the Antarctic: From Conquest to Modern Science* (Oslo, 2008), p. 49.
9 Ibid.
10 Cornelia Lüdecke and Colin Summerhayes, *The Third Reich in Antarctica: The German Antarctic Expedition, 1938–39* (Norwich and Huntingdon, 2012), p. 18.
11 Siple, *90° South*, p. 82.
12 H. R. Hall, 'The "Open Door" into Antarctica: An Explanation of the Hughes Doctrine', *Polar Record*, XXV (1989), pp. 137–40.
13 Christopher C. Joyner and Ethel R. Theis, *Eagle Over the Ice: The U.S. in the Antarctic* (Hanover, NH, and London, 1997), p. 40.
14 Jean Robert Petit, 'The Vostok Venture: An Outcome of the Antarctic Treaty', in *Science Diplomacy*, ed. Paul Arthur Berkman et al. (Washington, DC, 2011), p. 166.
15 Dodds, *The Antarctic*, p. 58.
16 Ibid., p. 67.
17 Quoted in Frank G. Klotz, *America on the Ice: Antarctic Policy Issues* (Washington, DC, 1990), p. 171.
18 Ibid., p. 191.
19 PDD/NSC-26, 'U.S. Antarctic Policy', available at www.fas.org.
20 Tim Wirth, in the *Rocky Mountain News*, quoted in Bernadette Hince, *The Antarctic Dictionary: A Complete Guide to Antarctic English* (Collingwood, Vic, 2000), p. 338.
21 Dodds, *The Antarctic*, p. 68.
22 Stephen Moss, 'No, It's Not a Ski Resort – It's the South Pole', *The Guardian* (24 January 2003), available at www.theguardian.com.

23 Malcolm W. Browne, 'Bold New Plan for Imperiled South Pole Station', *New York Times* (28 June 1994), p. C1. Bryon MacWilliams, 'Russia Pulls Out of Antarctic Station', *Nature*, CDXXII (13 March 2003), p. 104.
24 Jane Qui, 'China Builds Inland Antarctic Base', *Nature News* (8 January 2009), available at www.nature.com.
25 William J. Mills, *Exploring Polar Frontiers: A Historical Encyclopedia* (Santa Barbara, CA, and Oxford, 2003), vol. II, p. 539.
26 Matthew Beard, 'British Explorers Recount "Agony" of Pole Trek', *The Independent* (23 January 2007), p. 9.

9 Pictures of Nothingness

1 *Parade*, 14 October 1956, p. 43. I am indebted to Bill Spindler's website www.southpolestation.com for my knowledge of this image.
2 Rüdiger Joppien and Bernard Smith, *The Art of Captain Cook's Voyages* (Melbourne, 1985), p. 19.
3 Ibid., p. 17.
4 Stephen J. Pyne, *The Ice: A Journey to Antarctica* (New York, 1988), p. 160.
5 Nigel Gosling, *Gustave Doré* (Newton Abbot, Devon, 1973), pp. 23–8.
6 William L. Fox, 'Every New Thing: The Evolution of Artistic Technologies in the Antarctic; or, How Land Arts Came to the Ice', in *Far Field: Digital Culture, Climate Change, and the Poles*, ed. Jane Marsching and Andrea Polli (Bristol and Chicago, IL, 2012), p. 21.
7 Pyne, *The Ice*, p. 176.
8 Robert K. Headland, *A Chronology of Antarctic Exploration* (London, 2009), p. 224.
9 Kathryn Yusoff, 'Configuring the Field: Photography in Early Twentieth-Century Antarctic Exploration', in *New Spaces of Exploration: Geographies of Discovery in the Twentieth Century*, ed. Simon Naylor and James R. Ryan (London, 2010), p. 73.
10 Beau Riffenburgh, *Nimrod: Ernest Shackleton and the Extraordinary Story of the 1907–09 British Antarctic Expedition* (London, 2004), p. 184.
11 David M. Wilson, *The Lost Photographs of Captain Scott: Unseen Images from the Legendary Antarctic* (New York and London, 2011), p. 26; Ernest Shackleton, *The Heart of the Antarctic: Being the Story of the British Antarctic Expedition, 1907–1909* (New York, 1999), pp. 250, 343.
12 Fox, 'Every New Thing', p. 23.

13 Harald Østgaard Lund, 'The South Pole Photograph', in *Roald Amundsens Sydpolekspedisjon, 1910–1912* [booklet accompanying DVD] (Oslo, 2010), pp. 169, 171; Roland Huntford, ed., *The Amundsen Photographs* (London, 1987), p. 44.
14 Roald Amundsen, *The South Pole: An Account of the Norwegian Antarctic Expedition in the 'Fram', 1910–1912* (London, 1912), vol. II, p. 39.
15 Lund, 'The South Pole Photograph', pp. 167–8.
16 See Wilson, *The Lost Photographs of Captain Scott.*
17 Herbert Ponting, *The Great White South: Traveling with Robert F. Scott's Doomed South Pole Expedition* (New York, 2001), pp. 185–6.
18 Amundsen, *The South Pole*, vol. II, p. 2.
19 Pyne, *The Ice*, pp. 187–9, 201.
20 Klaus J. Dodds, 'Screening Antarctica: Britain, the Falkland Islands Dependencies Survey and *Scott of the Antarctic* (1948)', *Polar Record*, XXXVIII (2002), p. 6.
21 Allison Barrett Beaumont, 'The U.S. Naval Art of Arthur Beaumont', available at www.navyart.com, accessed 22 April 2015. Arthur Beaumont's Antarctic artworks can be seen at this website.
22 Emil Schulthess, *Antarctica*, trans. Peter Gorge (London, 1961), text accompanying pl. 96.
23 Pyne, *The Ice*, p. 194.
24 Rodney James, *Sidney Nolan: Antarctic Journey*, exh. cat., Mornington Peninsula Regional Gallery, Victoria (2006), pp. 7, 10.
25 Fox, 'Every New Thing', p. 23.
26 James, *Sidney Nolan*, p. 12.
27 Ibid., p. 37.
28 Ibid., p. 3.
29 Ibid., pp. 2–3.
30 Schulthess, *Antarctica*, text accompanying pl. 13; Eliot Porter, *Antarctica* (New York, 1978), p. 117.
31 Porter, *Antarctica*, p. 16.
32 Elena Glasberg, *Antarctica as Cultural Critique: The Gendered Politics of Scientific Exploration and Climate Change* (New York, 2012), pp. 90, 93.
33 Ibid., p. 90.
34 William L. Fox, 'Mirror from an Other World', in *The Antarctic: From the Circle to the Pole* (San Francisco, CA, 2008), p. 13.
35 Fox, 'Every New Thing', p. 24.
36 Glasberg, *Antarctica as Cultural Critique*, p. 102.
37 Michael Almereyda, 'An-My Lê' [interview transcript], *Bombsite: The Artists Voice since 1981*, available at http://bombsite.com, accessed 22 April 2015.

38 'An-My Lê: Events Ashore', press release available at the (New York gallery) Murray Guy website, http://murrayguy.com, accessed 22 April 2015.
39 Glasberg, *Antarctica as Cultural Critique*, p. 96.
40 Quoted in Mark Chalon Smith, 'Southern Exposures', *Today@UCI*, 7 June 2005, available at http://archive.today.uci.edu.
41 Samaras's *V.A.L.I.S.* series can be viewed online at her website www.conniesamaras.com.
42 Connie Samaras, 'American Dreams', *Scholar and Feminist Online*, VII/1 (Fall 2008), available at http://sfonline.barnard.edu., p. 1.
43 Ibid., p. 2.
44 Anne Noble, untitled note, *These Rough Notes*, by Bill Manhire, Anne Noble, Norman Meehan and Hannah Griffin (Wellington, 2012), p. 63.
45 Paul Coldwell, *Re-Imagining Scott: Objects and Journeys*, exh. cat., The Polar Museum, Scott Polar Research Institute (Cambridge, 2013), p. 22.
46 This and other South Pole installations by Cortada are described at his website, www.cortada.com.
47 Samaras, 'American Dreams', p. 1.

10 Adventurers and Extreme Tourists

1 Adventure Network International, '90° South Overnight', available at www.adventure-network.com, accessed 22 April 2015.
2 Robert K. Headland, *A Chronology of Antarctic Exploration: A Synopsis of Events and Activities from the Earliest Times until the International Polar Years, 2007–09* (London, 2009), p. 58. Many of the details of expeditions to the South Pole cited in this chapter are based on this work.
3 See Greg O'Brien, 'Towards an Antarctic Tourism Policy', Graduate Certificate in Antarctic Studies thesis, University of Canterbury, Christchurch (2009), p. 2, available at www.anta.canterbury.ac.nz.
4 Thomas G. Bauer, *Tourism in the Antarctic: Opportunities, Constraints, and Future Prospects* (Binghamton, NY, 2001), p. 15.
5 Carl Murray and Julia Jabour, 'Independent Expeditions and Antarctic Tourism Policy', *Polar Record*, XL (2004), p. 311.
6 Ranulph Fiennes, in Kari Herbert and Huw Lewis-Price, *In Search of the South Pole* (London, 2011), pp. 15, 17.
7 Dixie Dansercoer, *Polar Exploration: A Practical Handbook for North and South Pole Expeditions* (Milnthorpe, Cumbria, 2012), p. 32.
8 Nicholas Johnson, *Big Dead Place: Inside the Strange and Menacing World of Antarctica* (Los Angeles, CA, 2005), p. 91.

9 Quoted in Roger Mear and Robert Swan, *In the Footsteps of Scott* (London, 1987), p. 241.
10 Johnson, *Big Dead Place*, p. 83.
11 David Burke, *Moments of Terror: The Story of Antarctic Aviation* (Kensington, NSW, 1994), p. 290.
12 Ralf-Peter Martin and Reinhold Messner, 'Chronicle of Antarctic Expeditions', *One World Magazine*, available at www.oneworldmagazine.org, accessed 22 April 2015.
13 Robert K. Headland, 'Exotic Terrestrial Mammals in the Antarctic Regions', *Polar Record*, XLVIII (2012), p. 139.
14 Hilary Whiteman, 'Walking to the South Pole', CNN online (2008), available at http://edition.cnn.com.
15 Erling Kagge, in Herbert and Lewis-Jones, *In Search of the South Pole*, p. 168
16 Quoted in Herbert and Lewis-Jones, *In Search of the South Pole*, p. 165.
17 Will Gow, quoted in 'Descendants Finishing Job Shackleton Began', *New Zealand Herald* online (18 November 2008), available at www.nzherald.co.nz.
18 'South Pole 2011' online expedition diary, available at http://sorpolen2011.npolar.no.
19 Peter Rejcek, 'South Pole Anniversary' and 'A Sombre Salute', *Antarctic Sun* (15 December 2011 and 20 January 2012), available at http://antarcticsun.usap.gov.
20 Rejcek, 'A Sombre Salute'.
21 Rosamunde J. Reich, 'The Development of Antarctic Tourism', *Polar Record*, XX (1980), p. 210.
22 Charles Swithinbank, 'Airborne Tourism in the Antarctic', *Polar Record*, XXIX (1993), p. 108.
23 Adventure Network International, 'Our History', available at www.adventure-network.com, accessed 6 August 2015.
24 All quotations and prices cited here are taken from ANI's website, www.adventure-network.com, accessed 6 August 2015.
25 This quotation and the details above are taken from Musika Fahnsworth, 'Tragedy in Antarctica', and following comments, *Parachustist*, LII/6 (June 2011), available at http://parachutistonline.com.
26 Adventure Network International, 'Environmental Sustainability', and '90° South Overnight', available at www.adventure-network.com, accessed 22 April 2015.
27 Statistics are available from IAATO – see 'Associations and Websites' at the end of this book.
28 Swithinbank, 'Airborne Tourism', p. 109.
29 Jeff Rubin, *Antarctica* (Footscray, Vic, 2005), p. 276.

30 'South Pole Flight', White Desert website, available at www.white-desert.com.
31 Mark Nuttall, 'Narratives of History, Environment and Global Change: Expeditioner-tourists in Antarctica', in *Tourism and Change in Polar Regions: Climate, Environments, Experiences*, ed. Michael C. Hall and Jarkko Saarinen (London and New York, 2010), pp. 204, 208.
32 Johnson, *Big Dead Place*, pp. 83, 85.
33 Headland, *Chronology*, p. 58.
34 Joseph E. Murphy, *South to the Pole by Ski* (Saint Paul, MN, 1990), p. 41; original emphasis.
35 Catherine Hartley, *To the Poles without a Beard* (London, 2003), pp. 158, 250.

SELECT BIBLIOGRAPHY

The academic journals *Polar Record* and the *Polar Journal* contain many accessible articles relating to the South Pole. There are also numerous biographies of Amundsen, Scott, Shackleton, Byrd and other explorers that describe their polar journeys, as well as published diaries by various expedition members.

Amundsen, Roald, *The South Pole: An Account of the Norwegian Antarctic Expedition in the 'Fram', 1910–1912*, trans. A. G. Chater [1912] (London, 2002)

—, *The Roald Amundsen Diaries: The South Pole Expedition, 1910–1912*, ed. Geir O. Kløver (Oslo, 2010)

Andrews, Lynne, *Antarctic Eye: The Visual Journey* (Mount Rumney, Tasmania, 2007)

Burke, David, *Moments of Terror: The Story of Antarctic Aviation* (Kensington, NSW, 1994)

Byrd, Richard E., *Little America: Aerial Exploration in the Antarctic and the Flight to the South Pole* (London, 1931)

Cherry-Garrard, Apsley, *The Worst Journey in the World: Antarctic, 1910–13* (London, 1994)

Dodds, Klaus, *The Antarctic: A Very Short Introduction* (Oxford, 2012)

Fox, William L., *Terra Antarctica: Looking into the Emptiest Continent* (San Antonio, TX, 2005)

Fuchs, Vivian, *Antarctic Adventure: The Commonwealth Trans-Antarctic Expedition, 1955–58* (London, 1959)

Glasberg, Elena, *Antarctica as Cultural Critique: The Gendered Politics of Scientific Exploration and Climate Change* (New York, 2012)

Hartley, Catherine, *To the Poles Without a Beard* (London, 2003)

Headland, Robert Keith, *A Chronology of Antarctic Exploration: A Synopsis of Events and Activities from the Earliest Times until the International Polar Years, 2007–09* (London, 2009)

Herbert, Kari, and Huw Lewis-Jones, *In Search of the South Pole* (London, 2011)
Huntford, Roland, ed., *The Amundsen Photographs* (London, 1987)
Johnson, Nicholas, *Big Dead Place: Inside the Strange and Menacing World of Antarctica* (Los Angeles, CA, 2005)
Jones, Max, *The Last Great Quest: Captain Scott's Antarctic Sacrifice* (Oxford, 2003)
Leane, Elizabeth, *Antarctica in Fiction: Imaginative Narratives of the Far South* (Cambridge, 2012)
Lund, Harald Østgaard, and Siv Frøydis Berg, *Norske polarheltbilder, 1888–1929* (Oslo, 2011)
Manhire, Bill, ed., *The Wide White Page: Writers Imagine Antarctica* (Wellington, 2004)
Mear, Roger, and Robert Swan, *In the Footsteps of Scott* (London, 1987)
Mills, William J., *Exploring Polar Frontiers: A Historical Encyclopedia* (Santa Barbara, CA, and Oxford, 2003)
Nielsen, Jerry, with Maryanne Vollers, *Ice Bound: A Doctor's Incredible Battle for Survival at the South Pole* (London, 2001)
Ponting, Herbert, *The Great White South: Traveling with Robert F. Scott's Doomed South Pole Expedition* (New York, 2001)
Riffenburgh, Beau, ed., *Encyclopedia of the Antarctica* (New York, 2007)
Rubin, Jeff, *Antarctica* [Lonely Planet Country Guide] (Footscray, Vic, 2005)
Scott, Robert F., *Journals: Captain Scott's Last Expedition*, ed. Max Jones (Oxford, 2006)
—, *The Voyage of the 'Discovery'* (Stroud, Gloucestershire, 2005)
Shackleton, Ernest, *The Heart of the Antarctic: Being the Story of the British Antarctic Expedition, 1907–1909* (New York, 1999)
Siple, Paul, *90° South: The Story of the American South Pole Conquest* (New York, 1959)
Spufford, Francis, *I May Be Some Time: Ice and the English Imagination* (London, 1996)
Turner, Gillian, *North Pole, South Pole: The Epic Quest to Solve the Great Mystery of Earth's Magnetism* (Wellington, NZ, 2010)
Walker, Gabrielle, *Antarctica: An Intimate Portrait of the World's Most Mysterious Continent* (London, 2012)
Walton, David W. H., ed., *Antarctica: Global Science from a Frozen Continent* (Cambridge, 2013)
Wilson, David M., *The Lost Photographs of Captain Scott* (London, 2011)

ASSOCIATIONS AND WEBSITES

Adventure Network International
www.adventure-network.com

Amundsen-Scott South Pole Station (Bill Spindler's Antarctica)
www.southpolestation.com

Antarctic Circle
www.antarctic-circle.org

Antarctic Sun: News about Antarctica
antarcticsun.usap.gov

Finding Antarctica: Mapping the Last Continent
www.sl.nsw.gov.au/events/exhibitions/2011/finding_antarctica

Fram Museum
www.frammuseum.no

International Association of Antarctic Tour Operators
iaato.org

Laura Kay's Polar Collections
www.phys.barnard.edu/~kay/polar

National Library of Norway (Nasjonalbiblioteket)
www.nb.no/english

Representations of Antarctica
www.utas.edu.au/representations-of-antarctica

Scott Polar Research Institute Library
www.spri.cam.ac.uk/library

South Pole Live Camera (National Oceanic and Atmospheric Administration)
www.esrl.noaa.gov/gmd/obop/spo/livecamera.html

U.S. South Pole Station (National Science Foundation)
www.nsf.gov/news/special_reports/livingsouthpole

ACKNOWLEDGEMENTS

This book was supported by the Australian Research Council under project FT120100402; and by the University of Tasmania, which provided funding through the Faculty of Arts Environment Research Group, the Institute for the Study of Social Change, the 'Rising Stars' programme, and its conference travel schemes, and also gave me a period of research leave. Due to this funding, I was able to benefit at different stages of the project from the work of two excellent research assistants, Anna Lucas and Bridget Eltham. I am very grateful for all of this support.

Like all books in the Earth series, *South Pole* ranges over a wide variety of subjects, and I am indebted to a large number of people for reading sections of the text, advising on particular topics, discussing chapters with me, pointing me to resources, or lending me their expertise in other ways. They include Andrew Atkin, Gordon Bain, Gary Burns, Dirk Couprie, Richard Collins, Ralph Crane, Carol Devine, Mark Duldig, Lisa Fletcher, Marcus Haward, Roslynn Haynes, Alan Hemmings, Stuart Klipper, Geir Kløver, Daniela Liggett, Graeme Miles, Paul Morin, David Neilson, Dave Neudegg, Steve Nicol, Heath O'Connell, Bill Spindler and Rupert Summerson. Needless to say, none should be held responsible for any errors, misinterpretations or subjective opinions expressed in this book, which are mine alone. Several people living at or travelling to the South Pole while I was writing this book provided images and information; I would especially like to thank Dale Molé and Wilson (Wai-Yin) Cheung. A number of photographers and fine artists very generously gave me permission to use their images; they are all listed in the Photo Acknowledgements. Richard Williams at the University of Tasmania took a series of photographs at my request, and I am grateful to him for his time, effort and skill. Curators and archivists at the Scott Polar Research Institute, the National Science Foundation and the Australian Antarctic Division, as well as a number of other institutes and image collections, were very helpful. I'd particularly like to thank Anne Melgård, Harald Østgaard Lund, Siv Frøydis Berg and Jens Petter Kollhøj at the Nasjonalbiblioteket in Norway for their hospitality, interest and advice.

Reaktion Books have made the publication process a straightforward and pleasant experience. I would like to acknowledge in particular Daniel Allen, Michael Leaman, Harry Gilonis and Amy Salter. Barbara Bessant provided timely assistance with aspects of the production process.

My family and friends were supportive and encouraging as ever during the writing of the book. Sally O'Connor and Michi Watkins gave practical help in many instances. My parents Peter and Christine Leane were terrific proofreaders and my husband Damian Murphy provided valuable advice, scientific and otherwise. My children Zachary and Tessa, who are always a delight, put up with my occasional distractedness. They now know that polar bears do not live at the South Pole, but I suspect they would find the book more exciting if they did. *South Pole* is dedicated to them.

PHOTO ACKNOWLEDGEMENTS

The author and publishers wish to express their thanks to the below sources of illustrative material and/or permission to reproduce it. Locations of some artworks not listed in the captions for reasons of brevity are also given below.

From *Aftenposten* 10 September 1912, photo reproduced courtesy of the National Library of Norway, Oslo: p. 158; Alexander Turnbull Library, Wellington, New Zealand: pp. 68 (Box 11, ref. PAColl-6504-44), 78 (Ref. Eph-F-ANTARCTICA-1930-01 – *Admiral Byrd's South Pole Game*; Reg. U.S. Patent Office. Parker Bros Inc.); Roald Amundsen, *Sydpolen*, vol. II (Kristiania, 1912), courtesy of National Library of Norway, Oslo: p. 57; from Victor Appleton II, *Tom Swift and his Atomic Earth Blaster*, illus. J. Graham Kaye (New York, 1954): p. 49; courtesy of the Australian Antarctic Division © Commonwealth of Australia: pp. 6 (February 2007), 139 (November 2008); Australian Antarctic Territory stamp images © Australian Postal Corporation: p. 146 (lower pair of images); photo Forest Banks, courtesy of National Science Foundation: p. 88; photo Alberto Behar (PhD) – NASA/ JPL/Caltech/NSF: p. 129; Andreas Bloch, *Norges flag plantet paa Sydpolen 13/12/1911* – Mittet & Co. Kunstforlag, Wilse Foto Eneret – courtesy of Norwegian National Library, Oslo: p. 141; courtesy of Phillipe Boissonnet: pp. 38–9; photo Dale Budd, courtesy of David Burke: p. 63; photo Gary Burns: p. 144; photos © Wai-Yin (Wilson) Cheung: pp. 93, 100–101, 108–9, 113, 116, 119, 175, 188, 189, 190, 191, 192, 193, 196–7; © Paul Coldwell: p. 172; image by Davepape using public domain NASA Blue Marble data: p. 26; NASA /Goddard Space Flight Center Scientific Visualization Studio [Blue Marble data courtesy of Reto Stockli (NASA/GSFC)]: p. 126; Zina Deretsky, National Science Foundation: p. 86, 102 (top); photos Jeremy Dillon, courtesy of Kirsten Haydon: pp. 154 (top), 155; ESO (European Southern Observatory)/F. Char: p. 19; from Wolcott Gibbs, *Bird Life at the Pole* (New York, 1931): p. 176; from Joseph Hall, *Mundus alter et idem: sive Terra Australis antehac semper incognita . . .*

(Vltraiecti [Utrecht], 1643), courtesy of the Rare Books Collection, State Library of Victoria, Melbourne: p. 46; photo Helmer Hanssen, Courtesy of National Library of Norway (bldsa_NPRA0534): p. 14 (top); from *Harper's New Monthly Magazine*, vol. LXV/389 (October 1882): p. 35; photo Jan Haug, The Royal Court, Oslo: p. 13 (bottom left); photo Weeks Heist: p. 103; photo Patrick Hovey, National Science Foundation: p. 128; photos James Dana Hrubes: pp. 104, 131, 132; from Jules S. C. Dumont d'Urville, *Voyage au Pôle Sud et dans l'Océanie sur les corvettes l'*Astrolabe *et la* Zélée*: exécuté* [. . .] *pendant les années 1837–1840, sous le commandement de M. J. Dumont d'Urville* . . ., vol. I (Paris, 1842), photo Steve Nicklas, NOS, NGS, courtesy of National Oceanic and Atmospheric Administration/U.S. Department of Commerce: p. 58; from William Earl Johns, *Biggles Breaks the Silence*, illus. Leslie Stead (London, 1948): p. 48; from W.H.G. Kingston, *At the South Pole* (London, 1882): p. 52; courtesy of Stuart Klipper: p. 164; © An-My Lê, courtesy Murray Guy, New York: p. 165; photos Library of Congress, Washington, DC: pp. 65, 66 (from *Puck*, vol. LXVI/1702, 13 October 1909); photo Jürgen Lübeck: p. 184; photo by Bill McAfee, National Science Foundation: p. 111; photo courtesy of Frederick McDougall: p. 182; photos Marie McLane: pp. 87, 170–71; *Mercator Map of the World*, by Ernest Dudley Chase (Boston: Houghton Mifflin, 1931) – used by permission, all rights reserved – Image courtesy of the David Rumsey Map Collection, www.davidrumsey.com: p. 29; photos Dale M. Molé: pp. 89, 120, 130; photo Steve Morgan/Greenpeace: p. 147; photos Damian Murphy: pp. 116–17, 118; images courtesy NASA: pp. 43, 114, 122–3; photos National Library of Australia, Canberra: pp. 16 (*Party at the South Pole, 18 January 1912* – nla.pic-vn4087833), 157 top (Olav Bjaaland, *The Successful Explorers at the South Pole, 14th December 1911* – nla.pic-an23814300); National Library of Norway, Oslo: pp. 13 – top and bottom right (NB Ms.4° 2730), 14 top (bldsa_ npra0524); National Library of Scotland, Edinburgh: p. 71; photo National Library of Sweden (Kungliga biblioteket), Stockholm, courtesy Christer Rohman: p. 79 (right); photo National Oceanic and Atmospheric Administration, U.S. Department of Commerce: p. 85; image Dennis Nilsson, including a public domain image from NASA– licensed under the Creative Commons Attribution 3.0 Unported license – any reader is free to share – to copy, distribute and transmit this composite work, or to remix – to adapt this composite work, under the following condition of attribution – you must attribute the work in the manner specified by the author or licensor (but not in any way that suggests that they endorse you or your use of the work): p. 21; NOAA's National Geophysical Data Center, December 2005 – Pole Location Data from UFM and IGRF-10 Magnetic Field Model: p. 24; © Anne Noble: pp. 168, 169, 187; photo courtesy of Alice O'Connor, supplied by the National Snow and Ice Data Center, University of Colorado, Boulder: p. 105; from *Parade*, 14 October 1956, reproduced courtesy of Sandra Scott: p. 153;

photo Joe Phillips, National Science Foundation: p. 148; courtesy of Posten Norge: p. 146 (upper pair of images); private collection – Photo © Agnew's, London/Bridgeman Images: p. 162; Nicolle Rager-Fuller, National Science Foundation: p. 99; from James Clark Ross, *A Voyage of Discovery and Research in the Southern and Antarctic Regions during the years 1839–43* . . ., vol. II (London, 1847): p. 59; courtesy the Royal Geographical Society (with the Institute of British Geographers): pp. 64, 79 (left), 157 (bottom); © Connie Samaras: pp. 166, 167; photo Ted Scambos, National Snow and Ice Data Center, University of Colorado, Boulder: p. 95; photo Ted Scambos and Rob Bauer, National Snow and Ice Data Center, University of Colorado, Boulder: p. 135; photo Liesl Schernthanner, National Science Foundation: p. 17; photo © Darryn Schneider/Dreamstime.com: p. 177; photo Robert Schwarz: p. 102 (foot); © Pierre R. Schwob – By Permission: p. 9; Scott Polar Research Institute, Cambridge: pp. 69, 72, 115, 154 (foot), 159; Courtesy the Shell Art Collection/Shell Brands International AG: p. 70; photo courtesy Geoff Somers: p. 186; from *The Sphere* 23 December 1911 (photo © British Library Board): p. 15; image courtesy of Andy Smith – originally published in Kari Herbert and Huw Lewis-Jones, *In Search of the South Pole* (London: Conway, 2011): p. 42; courtesy of Bill Spindler: p. 14 (bottom); from Gordon Stables, *In the Great White Land: A Tale of the Antarctic Ocean*, illus. Ambrose de Walton (London, n. d. [1st edn 1903]): p. 53; State Library of New South Wales, Sydney: pp. 30 (Call no. MRB/X910/10), 31 (Call no. MRB/Q878.9/M), 32 (Call no. Q53/2); courtesy of the State Library of South Australia, Adelaide: p. 62; photo Craig Stevens, courtesy of National Institute of Water and Atmosphere Research (NIWA), New Zealand: pp. 106–7; photo Deven Stross, National Science Foundation: p. 145; courtesy of Rupert Summerson: p. 150; from *Tidens Tegn*, reproduced courtesy of the National Library of Norway, Oslo: pp. 8 (9 March 1912), 156 (16 May 1912); photo Stein Tronstad, courtesy of Norwegian Polar Institute: p. 151; photo Francis Vallance, licensed under the Creative Commons Attribution 2.0 Generic license – any reader is free to share – to copy, distribute and transmit this work, or to remix – to adapt this work - under the following condition of attribution – you must attribute the work in the manner specified by the author or licensor (but not in any way that suggests that they endorse you or your use of the work): p. 74; from Jules Verne, *Vingt mille mieues sous les mers* (Paris, 1870): p. 45; photo Keith Vanderlinde / University of Toronto: p. 110; photo RADM David F. (Kelly) Welch, courtesy of Bill Spindler: p. 90; Richard Williams: pp. 41, 56, 76, 77.

INDEX